BENJAMIN PERET
(1899-1959)

In this world of specialists and appointed robots, a man of truth is an archaism. If our time is that of nihilism, as certain people pretend it to be, Benjamin Péret, man of hope, is a figure of the past. But is this not at the same time the proof that he is the man and poet of the future?

— **Octavio Paz**

∅

....A force of purer quality than the one the poetry of Péret possesses does not exist in or outside surrealism.

— **Nicolas Calas**

∅

Marcel Noll: "What is Benjamin Péret?"
Raymond Queneau: "A menagerie in revolt, a jungle, liberty."
("Dialogue in 1928", in *La révolution surréaliste*)

Surrealist Editions
BLACK SWAN PRESS

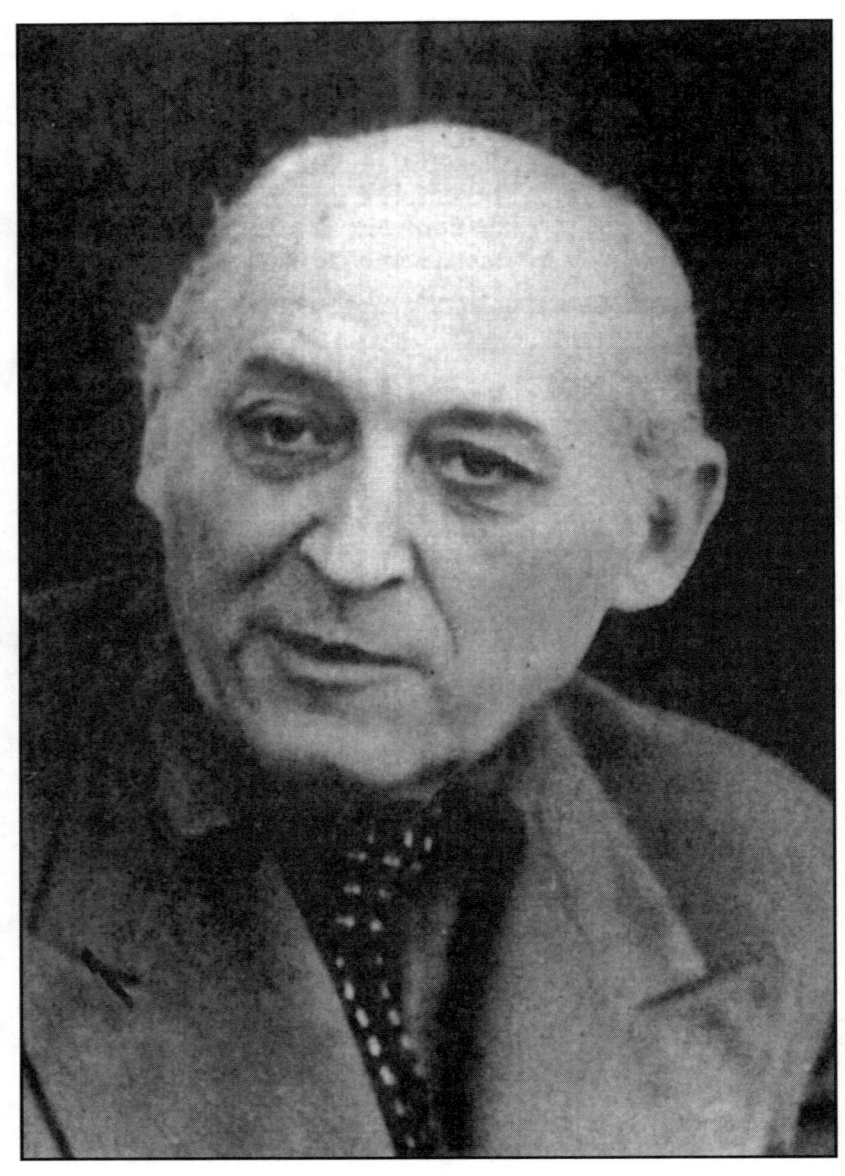

Benjamin Pèret

Benjamin Péret

A MENAGERIE IN REVOLT

Selected Writings

Introduced by Franklin Rosemont

With an Afterword by Don LaCoss

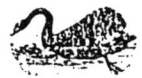

Surrealist Editions

BLACK SWAN PRESS

2009

Acknowledgments:
The Charles H. Kerr Company would like to thank
Benjamin Pèret's son, Geyser Pèret and his family,
especially his daughters Jacqueline and Sandra for help and
permission to publish the writings in this book.
Thanks also to Mary Low, Grandizo Munis, Al Glotzer,
Daniel Guérin, Amanda Armstrong, Madeleine Arenivar,
Ngo Van and Hélène Fleury for their assistance.

First Edition

ISBN old system: 0-88286-299-5
ISBN new system: 978-0-88286-299-6

Distributed by:
Charles H. Kerr Publishing Company
1726 West Jarvis Avenue
Chicago, Il 60626

TABLE OF CONTENTS

PREFACE

The purpose of this book is to provide a representative collection of writings—essays, theory, polemic, poetry and stories—by Benjamin Péret, one of international surrealism's outstanding figures.

Like so many books, this one has a history. It originally appeared in August 1970 as a 28-page section of *Radical America*, the leading journal of the Students for a Democratic Society (SDS), published in Madison, Wisconsin and edited by Paul Buhle. The entire 28-page section has been reprinted several times over the years, and, for better or for worse, my nine-page "Introduction" has been reprinted several times more.

In this new, expanded edition, I have decided to let the original introduction remain for the most part intact, excesses and all. My style back then (in my mid-twenties) was lush with adverbs and clauses in the French style I so admired. I like to think that the information given remains relevant to the understanding of Péret and his ongoing influence.

I have loved Péret since my first encounter with his work, when I was 15. I recall exactly the place I was sitting in a class, listening to the droning of a very boring teacher. Then, leafing through *The Reader's Companion to World Literature* I found the entry on surrealism. What stood before me was the proverb by Péret and Eluard: "elephants are contagious." I laughed and laughed. I'm sure elephants are even more contagious today than they were then, since our consciousness of the natural world and its beings has multiplied. I hope the following pages will expand your imagination even more.

Franklin Rosemont
Chicago, 2008

RADICAL
AMERICA

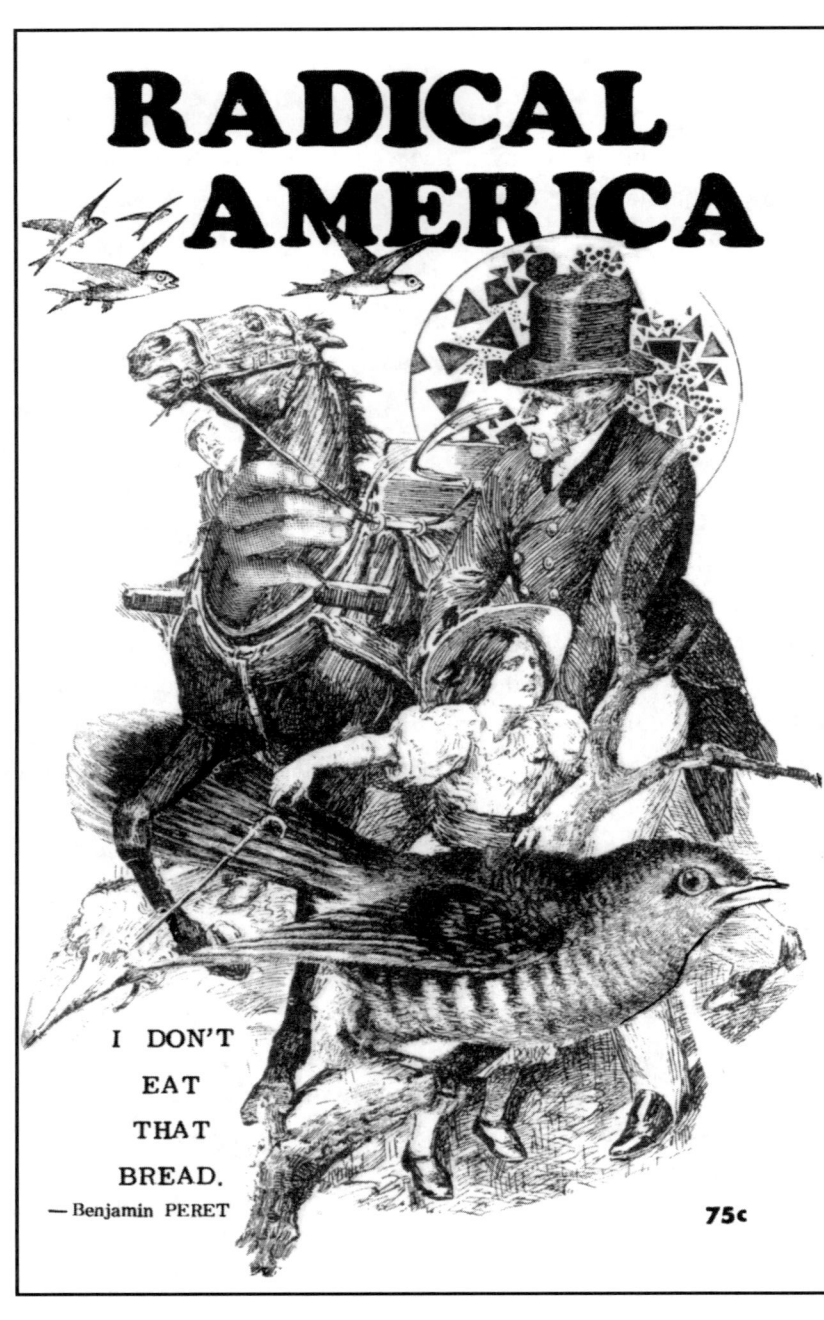

I DON'T
EAT
THAT
BREAD.
— Benjamin PERET

75¢

INTRODUCTION TO THE READING OF
BENJAMIN PERET

Franklin Rosemont

Marcel Noll: "What is Benjamin Péret?"
Raymond Queneau: "A menagerie in revolt, a jungle, liberty."
("Dialogue in 1928," in La Révolution Surréaliste*)*

The destiny of Benjamin Péret, at once poignantly heroic and wildly innocent, is something I continue to find immeasurably moving. It is doubtless impossible to convey anything more than the very slightest impression of the vertiginous intellectual joy which I experienced as I discovered, around the age of seventeen, the photograph of Péret in the eighth issue of *La Révolution Surréaliste* captioned: "Our Collaborator Benjamin Péret Insulting a Priest." But this simple encounter, which may seem trivial, was nonetheless decisive for me. The straw lions of Truth and the wooden ostriches of Beauty rushed together, thoroughly combustible, across the pale vicissitudes of everyday life, leaving in their ravaged wake of ashes a trail of immense possibilities which, irresistibly, I began to follow wherever it might lead. This path, moreover, has never disappointed me....

Péret is one of those few men whose entire lives have been given over to the cause of human emancipation. There is not a line in his work which does not pulsate with this profound passion for freedom.

In the history of surrealism Péret holds, securely, a position of the first rank.[1] He had participated in the activities of Dada in Paris, and was one of the first to advance beyond the limitations of this movement into the more subversive terrain of surrealism. He is, in fact, with René Crevel and Robert Desnos, one of the central pillars and reference-points of the "period of sleeping fits," the months of intensive experimentation with hypnotic trances immediately preceding the establishment of surrealism as an organized movement. We find his name among those cited in the first *Surrealist Manifesto* of 1924 as having proclaimed "Absolute Surrealism." The same year, with Pierre Naville, he edited the first issue of *La Révolution Surréaliste*. His published works of these years possess an exalted and exalting grandeur and vitality which, almost half a century later, have lost none of their illuminating force.

For critics, it is sufficient to pretend 1) that surrealism's internecine quarrels were and are of no importance; 2) that the "function" of surrealism has been to serve as an adolescent training-ground in which poets like Aragon, Eluard, and Char first found their voice; and 3) that these gentlemen wrote their truly "great" poetry only after renouncing surrealism. The time is long overdue when such imbecile contentions must be hurled into the flames of laughter to perish once and for all. Excuse us if we state simply and sincerely that the post-surrealist exercises of Aragon, Eluard, and Char constitute nothing more than a surrender to the basest literary vanity and complacency which has absolutely nothing to do with the emancipatory character of authentic poetic practice. Excuse us if we see in the later work of these gentlemen only a series of boring regressions, a senile return to the safe and protective womb of literary convention. (As Nicolas Calas wrote a propos Aragon's novels of the late '30s—so different from his incredible surrealist *Le Paysan de Paris* of the preceding decade: "...it seems to me that if one wishes to read novels in the manner of Balzac one should take the trouble to go back to the masters and not be satisfied with imitations such as those offered by Aragon. The return to a pre-surrealist position does not solve the problems of modern poetry."[2]) Excuse us, finally, if we insist that a single line by Benjamin Péret is worth every "post-surrealist" apology that ever was or will be.

Benjamin Péret never once succumbed to the conformist temptations which eventually brought so many of the companions of his youth into the camp of literary Law and Order. Marvelously uncompromising to the very end, we find him writing in 1959—the year of his death at the age of sixty—such amazingly youthful lines as these:

> *"a sigh cut across by the rumble of drums*
> *and the raucous cries of insane tables*
> *at grips with the fury of physical laws*
> *more intolerant than a wagon of Jesuits*
> *painted in two colors."*
>
> (from "Sign of the Times")

The unextinguishable impenitence and intransigence which characterizes Péret's intervention in the domain of poetry is no less characteristic of his intervention in the domain of politics. Completely against the fashionable current according to which radical intellectuals are supposed, sooner or later, to "return to the fold," to "outgrow" the revolutionary proclivities of their youth, Péret's entire life was lived "in the service of the Revolution." He is one of the five (with Aragon, Breton, Eluard, and Unik) who, in 1927, in the pamphlet *Au Grand Jour*, declared their adhesion, as surrealists and militants, to the French Communist Party.

Shortly afterward, in Brazil (whither he had moved with his Brazilian wife), he adhered to the Liga Communista (OpposiÇao), affiliated with the international Left Opposition. It was his revolutionary activity which led to his incarceration and expulsion from Brazil by the government in 1931.

In 1936 he was in Spain fighting as a militiaman for the proletarian revolution against the fascist counter-revolution, its bourgeois support, and the betrayal of the workers by the Stalinists and the anarchist leaders. In these years Péret, like the entire surrealist movement (and like so many other honest revolutionaries of the 1930s, revolted by the monstrous bureaucratic degeneration of the Russian Revolution in the hands of Stalin and his faction) made no secret of his sympathy for Leon Trotsky, for the Left Opposition, for the cause of genuine Leninism, for workers' power. He participated in the International Federation for an Independent Revolutionary Art (FIARI) inaugurated in 1938 by a manifesto written by Trotsky and André Breton.

Throughout the Second World War he was active in revolutionary activity in Mexico. In 1945, in a group which shortly afterward included Natalia Trotsky, Péret resigned from the Fourth International, mostly because of its theoretical and practical decline after the murder of Trotsky, but also in keeping with Trotsky's own pronouncements regarding the necessity of completely rethinking Marxist theory if socialist revolution did not emerge from the Second World War. This departure by Péret by no means indicated political retirement. His subsequent activity in the realm of politics is given primarily to the re-examination of important theoretical questions and insufficiently studied episodes of revolutionary history.

In this sense Péret's last political efforts could be said to parallel certain aspects of the work of *Informations Correspondance Ouvrières, Socialisme ou Barbarie*, the London *Solidarity* group, Herbert Marcuse, C.L.R. James, Raya Dunayevskaya and others whose critical revaluations of the past remain of considerable importance in the forging of a new revolutionary theory and practice today. No one can pretend that

4

any of these groups or individuals has found more than a small portion of the revolutionary truth necessary for the development of a movement capable of truly overthrowing the capitalist order and inaugurating "the kingdom of freedom."

But against a background of Stalinist defamation and lies, social-democratic senility, sectarian irrelevance and new left pompousness, it is especially important to explore the testimony of those who pursued independent courses against the grain of the general stagnation and defeat. It is essential to learn what can be learned from them, to understand which of their efforts can be considered advances, as well as which are merely retreats. What must be avoided at all costs is the dogmatic, essentially religious spirit of simple-minded pseudo-critical complete acceptance or rejection. Lenin's critical remarks, in his *Philosophical Notebooks*, on the relative superficiality of Plekhanov are clearly applicable in this regard. "Plekhanov criticizes Kantianism (and agnosticism in general)," Lenin writes, "more from a vulgar-materialistic standpoint, insofar as he merely rejects their views from the threshold, but does not correct them (as Hegel corrected Kant), deepening, generalizing, and extending them, showing the connection and transitions of each and every concept." In order to supersede the weaknesses and shortcomings of earlier efforts, it is necessary to critically assimilate their real contributions.

Péret's contributions, moreover, possess a dimension lacking in the work of his more narrowly political contemporaries. It is John Reed who once claimed to have found the thread that united cubism and the Industrial Workers of the World. A still more marvelous thread runs through the life of Benjamin Péret uniting the permanent revelation of surrealism to the permanent revolution of the working class: a double adherence to the revolutionary cause which gives Péret's entire poetic and political message a special resonance today.

Let us single out, from Péret's many political writings from this last period, a few which are of particular interest: a series of articles on labor unions published in *Libertaire*, in one section of which he defends certain conceptions of the little-known Dutch Marxist Hermann Gorter;[3] his review of Trotsky's autobiography in *Médium: Communication Surréaliste*, in which he discusses, among other things, the urgent significance of the Spanish Revolution;[4] and his small book (forbidden to be advertised in France) *Pour Un Second Manifeste Communiste*, written in collaboration with Grandizo Munis.[5] This last work, the point of departure of which is a critique of the post-war degeneration of the Fourth International, and which also contains a brief survey of the evolution of modern capitalism, calls for a "trenchant break with dead tactics and dead ideas" and for the elaboration of a "program of demands in accord with the maximum possibilities of modern technology and culture put in the service of humanity".

The most vital and revolutionary currents in modern poetry owe much to Benjamin Péret. The appearance of his work in English translation[6] is especially welcome since Péret's characteristic aggressivity, revolt, and humor, as well as his admirably incurable passion for all that is marvelous, are precisely the qualities most lacking in poetry in the English language in this century. (One would have to go to Blake's *Island in the Moon* or to certain works of Lewis Carroll: *The Hunting of the Snark*, for example, or the songs of the gardener in *Sylvie and Bruno*, to approach, in English, the poetic universe of Péret.) André Breton, in his *Anthologie de l'Humour Noir*, has described the great poetic advance made by Péret. Before him the greatest poets in the French language had been able to see only "a mosque in place of a factory" (Rimbaud) or to see "a fig eating a donkey" (Lautréamont). Moreover, "...they seem to

6

hold to the sentiment that they are committing a violation, that they are profaning human consciousness, that they are infringing on the most sacred of taboos. With Benjamin Péret, to the contrary, this sort of 'bad conscience' is done away with, censorship no longer exerts itself, one pleads that 'all is permitted.'"[7] For example:

"*I call tobacco that which is ear*
and the mites take their chance to throw themselves on the ham
hence a remarkable fight between the springs
flowing from gingerbread
and the spectacles that prevent blind men from seeing clearly"
(from "Who is it?")

It must be emphasized that Péret is, far more than is generally thought, a poet of love. But love for Péret has nothing to do with conventional pseudo-amorous sentimentality nor the vile platitudes of so-called "popular" music: it is, rather, the most decisive and thoroughgoing individual human experience, comprising the most delirious and overpowering moments of one's life: love which is wild, succulent, corrosive, frenzied, violently opposed to constraint; love which, in a single glance, is capable of reinventing, from scratch, one's conceptions of life.

The poetry of Benjamin Péret, with its rapid and violent metamorphoses, its wild shattering flights, like a Roman candle, into the blue sky of appearances, and its mad plunges, like an uncontrollable bathysphere, into the deepest sea of dreams, seems to me especially well-equipped to disperse the stale mythological fog that still obscures man's desperate glance into the future, and to restore to man a truer vision of his infinite capacities for transforming the world. Long before reaching the second line, Péret has established the dictatorship of the imagination and rigorously enforces the revolutionary terror of the convulsively beautiful image.

The same may be said for another category of Péret's work, his considerable number of tales,[8] which are in fact really inseparable from the rest of his poetic practice. It goes without saying that these "prose" works are entirely independent of the various insignificant devices of fiction—plot, character development, setting, et cetera—literary gadgets which Péret turns against themselves in the service of a superior order of imaginative activity. Thus these narratives do not meet the ordinary definitions of a "short story," any more than the longer tales—some of which are of book length, and divided into chapters—may accurately be called "novels." The effect of these tales is like a fresh breath of pure oxygen in a musty room: one feels a certain exhilaration, a sense of expansiveness; one feels freer, surer of oneself, perhaps slightly dizzy—but it is a dizziness quite distinct from intoxication: it is the feeling of looking over a cliff at a great height which one is delighted to have reached. It is to Péret's everlasting credit that he continually reaches such heights, as far as possible from the mundane, that he does so without effort, and that he takes the reader along with him on these lyrical expeditions.

Alongside and allied with his poetry and tales is Péret's theoretical work, the importance of which, for surrealism, is immense. In *La Parole est à Péret*, *Le Déshonneur des Poètes*, "Thought is One and Indivisible," and "Noyau de Cométe," Péret explores, with verve and lucidity, the origins and development of the poetic faculties, their applications, implications, and ramifications. Always emphasizing the libratory essence of poetry, always defending the subversive primacy of love in the gamut of emotions, always celebrating the revolt of the mind against its jailers, he traces the trajectory of myths and legends, the perversions of religious mystification, the interrelationships between poetry and society, between poetry and revolution. These texts testify with burning clarity to Péret's relentless devotion to the cause of breaking the social, cultural, and psychological fetters which reduce the imagination to misery and degradation. "The poet of today," he wrote, "has no other choice than to be a revolutionist or not to be a poet."[9]

It was Péret's rare genius to be able to speak of revolutionary poetry and revolutionary politics equally from within. But let us hasten to add, to avoid a confusion of a fundamental point, that Péret consistently refused any false, arbitrary, superficial syntheses of these two complementary but independent planes of revolutionary activity. Unlike many current so-called "cultural revolutionaries," including the ideologists of various "avant-garde" sects who boast of having "surpassed" surrealism, and who proclaim that they are able to "solve" the problems of poetry and revolution, and all problems, with the mere application of a few convenient "anti-artistic" formulas, Péret disdained such evasive pretensions and invariably approached the burning questions of human freedom with full recognition of their complexity and diversity. The cause of the liberation of the mind (surrealism) and the cause of proletarian revolution (Marxism) are not at all, in the eyes of Péret, reducible to abstract philosophical schemes or readymade slogans. They represent, rather, concrete and miraculous moments in the struggle for the total liberation of man. "These two activities," as Jean Schuster has written, "for him, surely, were but one. But the lucidity of his consciousness permitted him to understand that an objective conciliation was premature. That is why, belonging to these two very close but separate movements, he strictly forbade himself to bend the course of one in terms of the essential principles or circumstantial imperatives of the other. That is why, in all serenity, he served, on two planes, revolutionary truth."[10]

Let us mention, briefly, certain other aspects of Péret's work.

His researches into the origins of poetry led him inevitably into the realm of anthropology. *La Parole est à Péret*, a veritable manifesto of surrealist poetry, was in fact written as an introduction to an anthology of pre-Columbian myths and legends. Péret visited with Indians in Mexico and in Brazil, and wrote some very interesting "Notes on Pre-Columbian Art."[11] He translated the Mayan *Book of Chilam Balam of Chumayel* into French, contributing to it an important introduction.[12] Here as in his other works one perceives the same remarkable freshness of vision, the same impassioned search for real significations beyond the surfaces of academic research.

Péret's *Anthologie de l'Amour Sublime*[13] is in many ways a counterpart of Breton's *Anthologie de l'Humour Noir*. (Is it not remarkable that Breton, theoretician of mad love, should compile an anthology of black humor, and that Péret, incomparable black humorist, should compile an anthology of sublime love?) He also prepared, in 1959, an extensive *Anthologie de la Poésie Surréaliste*, for which he wrote a militant introduction.[14]

He wrote many prefaces to exhibitions of surrealist painters, which, if collected, would make a marvelous small volume.[15] These essays—on Wifredo Lam, Jindrich Styrsky, Joan Miro, Victor Brauner, E. F. Granell, Toyen, and others— demonstrate Péret's masterful clairvoyance, his magnetic sensitivity to the most vibrant and electrifying currents in modern painting. Finally, it is touching to note that this author, so notorious for his alleged "incoherence", for his completely unpredictable verbal play, was employed, for a considerable period of his life, as a proofreader. The life of Benjamin Péret: a life—as his surrealist friends expressed it in their salutation to him in a preface to the original edition of *La Parole est à Péret* —"singularly pure of concessions."

For some of us, Benjamin Péret is one of the surest guides of the spirit through the labyrinths of contemporary confusion. Our fervent regard for his attitude of total subversion, for his exemplary poetic and revolutionary position, will doubtless seem to some professionally solemn ideologists to be exaggerated or even hysterical. But it is precisely these ideologists who reflect the incredible backwardness of this country in matters of poetry and revolutionary thought. Is it not agonizing to contemplate the great influence exerted, not so long ago, upon radicals in this country by a ludicrous mediocrity like Albert Camus, while the work of Breton and Péret went unnoticed?

Tom-Tom 1
For Benjamin Péret

Even the river of blood of land
Even the blood of the broken sun
Even the blood of a hundred nails of sun
Even the blood of suicide from the fire beasts
Even the blood of ash the blood of salt the blood
     From the bloods of love
Even the flaming blood of the fire bird
Herons and falcons
Rise and burn

              Aimé Césaire
             (translated by Cheryl Seaman)

Today of course it is the neo-stalinists, the structuralists of the Althusserian school, the watchdogs of sectarian sterility rather than defeated existentialists or sentimental social-democratic apologists such as Erich Fromm who cast the most somber shadows over the light which is only beginning to glimmer. I think the time has come, however, when it is necessary to put an end to this humorless farce. "Perseus wore a magic cap that the monsters he hunted down might not see him. We draw the magic cap down over eyes and ears as a make-believe that there are no monsters." So said Marx.[16] It is time, once and for all, to tear off the cap and confront the monsters.

What is called for now is the ability to look squarely at that from which almost everybody has until now turned aside: social, human reality in its complex totality. The time has come when the grimace of the existentialist, the pout of the structuralist, the expressionlessness of the Stalinist, the mindless uncritical grin of the hippie, the leer of the sectarian, the complacent shrug of the analyst, and the supercilious sneer of the "post-scarcity" anarchist ("Tics, tics, tics!" cried Lautréamont) must give way, definitively, to the tidal wave of scathing humor which alone can silence the death-knells of pseudo-theory, overpower the guards of the prison of alienation, open the floodgates of authentic inspiration, and return to man a proper sense of his revolutionary destiny.

It goes without saying that it is only in such an atmosphere of intellectual effervescence that the work of Benjamin Péret can find readers equal to its sublime message. So close to us, so astonishingly alive among us while so many others who are better known and more influential are actually little more than dead weights restraining the forward thrust, this man remains a beacon; the light he sheds is vast and second to none. To emerge from the cloisters of traditional thinking into Péret's black light of words is, to be sure, to take an extraordinary risk. But let no one who is afraid of such risks dare speak to us of freedom! In the quest for the Golden Fleece of the Revolution, he will be the loser who does not, sooner or later, encounter the illuminating, immortal, intractable, and irreducible genius of Benjamin Péret.

Chicago, 1970

Notes

1. The only full-length studies devoted to Péret have been written by surrealists. A biographical and bibliographical chronology of Péret's life and work may be found in Courtot, Pages 11-57. Also see: Jehan Mayoux, "Benjamin Péret: La Fourchette Coupante" in *Le Surréalisme, même*, Numbers 2 and 3 (1957); Jean-Louis Bédouin, *Benjamin Péret* (Paris, Seghers, 1961); and Claude Courtot, *Introduction à la Lecture de Benjamin Péret* (Paris, Le Terrain Vague, 1965). In English there is almost nothing: a preface by J. H. Matthews to his translations of twenty poems by Péret, entitled *Péret's Score* (Paris, Minard, 1965); a chapter in Matthews' *Surrealist Poetry in France* (Syracuse University Press, 1969); Matthews' article, "Mechanics of the Marvelous: The Short Stories of Benjamin Péret," in *L'Esprit Créateur* (VI, 1, 1966); an excerpt from Courtot's study in *Radical America* (January 1970); and a worthless article by Mary Ann Caws, "Péret: Plausible Surrealist," in *Yale French Studies* 31 (May 1964). Miss Caws is the author of another article on Péret ("Péret's Amour sublime—just another amour fou?" in *The French Review*, November 1966) which I have not seen; however, her most recent book, *The Poetry of Dada and Surrealism* (Princeton, 1970), from which she excludes Péret because "his theoretical work tends toward the simplistic" (Page 14), situates her clearly in the category of those who have nothing to say.
2. Nicolas Calas, *Confound the Wise* (New York, Arrow Editions, 1942), Chapter 1, "The Light of Words," Page 28. This chapter, incidentally, carries a dedication to Péret.
3. These articles, which originally appeared in 1952, have recently been collected, supplemented with an essay by Grandizo Munis and a preface by Jehan Mayoux, published under the title *Les Syndicats Contre la Révolution* (Paris, Le Terrain Vague, 1968).
4. "Sa Vie", in *Médium: Communication Surréaliste* 3, May 1954, Pages 32-36. "The Spanish Revolution," Péret writes, "has not been the

object of the attentive examination that it deserves." (He notes as an exception Grandizo Munis, "Jalones de derrota, promesa de victoria," *Editorial Lucha Obrera*, Mexico 1947.) "However, at its beginnings it had gone much farther than the Russian Revolution."

5. A small volume of 76 pages, published bilingually in French and Spanish by Le Terrain Vague, Paris, 1965, under the auspices of the group Fomento Obrero Revolucionario.

6. Two small volumes of Péret's poetry have appeared in English translation. The first, *Remove Your Hat* (London, Contemporary Poetry and Prose, 1936) is today quite scarce, but is scheduled to be reprinted by Black Swan Press. Matthews' volume is cited in Note 1 above. Translations of poems by Péret have also appeared in *This Quarter* (Surrealist Number, 1932); Julien Levy, *Surrealism* (New York, Black Sun Press, 1936); *New Directions* 1940, and in surrealist and surrealist-oriented periodicals such as *London Bulletin, View, Contemporary Poetry and Prose, Rebel Worker*, et cetera.

7. André Breton, *Anthologie de l'Humour Noir* (Paris, Pauvert, 1966), Page 506.

8. Péret's tales, in French, were collected under the title *Le Gigot: Sa Vie, Son Oeuvre* (Paris, Le Terrain Vague, 1957). The first volume of Péret's *Oeuvres Complètes* has just been published by Le Terrain Vague. In English see "At 125, Boulevard Saint-Germain" in *This Quarter* (Surrealist Number, 1932); "In a Clinch," in *Transition* 12, later in *Transition Workshop* (New York, Vanguard Press, 1949); "The Gallant Sheep," Chapter 4, in *Radical America*, Surrealist Number, Jan., 1970.

9. "Magic: The Flesh and Blood of Poetry," in *View* (Series 3, Number 2, 1943). This is a slightly abridged translation of *La Parole est à Péret*. It was recently reprinted in *Antinarcissus: Surrealist Conquest*, an anthology published in San Francisco. Also see "Thought is One and Indivisible," in *Surrealism and Revolution* (Chicago, Solidarity, 1966).

10. Jean Schuster, "Profil de Péret," introduction to the most recent edition of Péret's *Le Déshonneur des poètes* (Paris, Pauvert, 1965), Pages 16 and 17.

11. "Notes on Pre-Columbian Art," in *Horizon* (Volume 15, Number 89, 1947).

12. *Livre de Chilam Balam de Chumayel* (Paris, Denoel, 1955).

13. *Anthologie de l'Amour Sublime* (Paris, Albin Michel, 1956).

14. *La Poesia surrealista francese* (Milan, Schwarz, 1959).

15. See also Péret's critique of abstract art, "La soupe deshydratée" in the *Almanach Surréaliste du demi-seicle*, special issue of La Nef, 1950.

16. Karl Marx, *Capital*, Volume I (Chicago, Charles H. Kerr and Company, 1906), Preface, page 14.

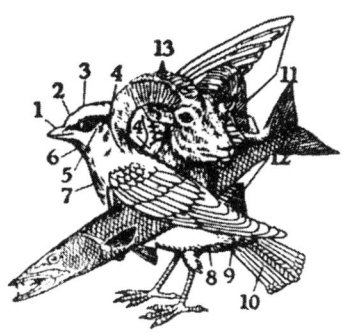

A MENAGERIE IN REVOLT

Benjamin Péret

The life of Benjamin Péret: a life "singularly
pure of concessions."
— Preface to the original edition of
La Parole est à Péret

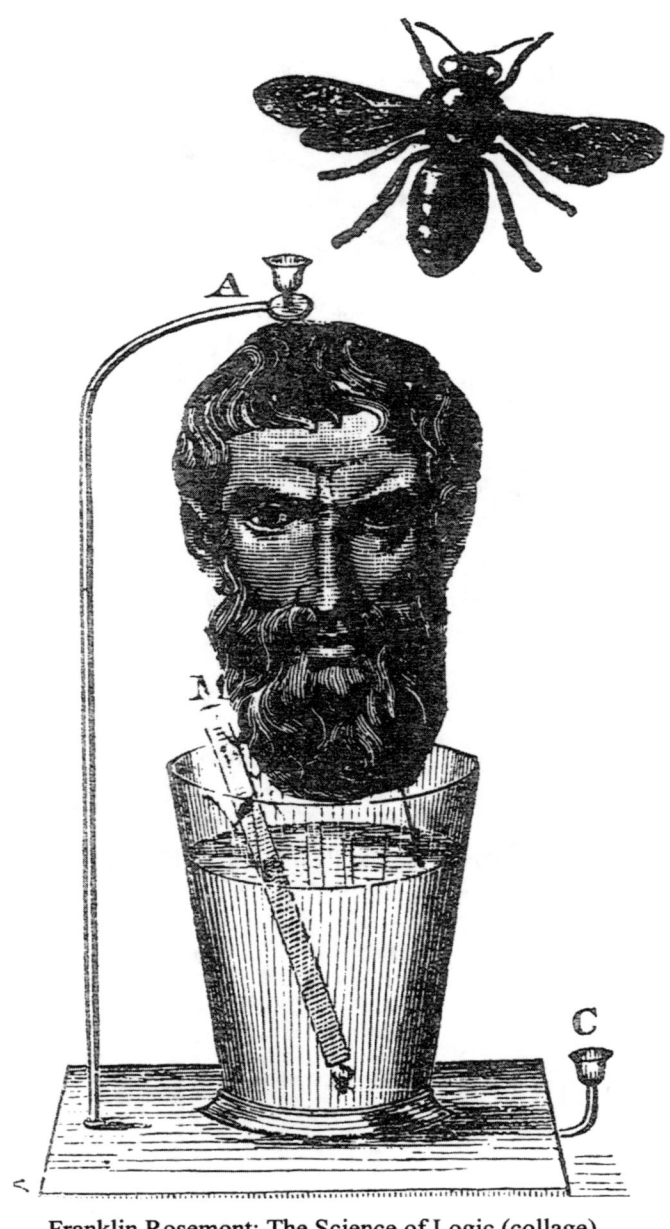

Franklin Rosemont: The Science of Logic (collage)

THE REMEMBRANCE OF THINGS TO COME

The raw art of popular consciousness in Mexico

N O PEOPLE IN THE WORLD, as primitive as they may be, lives without poetry, for poetry is the natural mode of thought of all mankind. I say "no people" for what is lost as a result of the elite's decline and failure to renew itself rises again among the masses, a coarse soil out of which sumptuous flowers may grow—the greatest cultures. Art, the plastic expression of this poetry, requires mastery of the material world, and thus takes time to evolve. Looked at in this way, Mexico offers the fascinating sight of a people whose culture, brutally razed by the Spanish conquest, seeks to rise again, as a lightning-amputated tree sprouts new twigs as soon as spring comes around. Alas, through no fault of its own, the Mexican springtime is contemporary with the autumn of the world. A reflection not on the spring, but on the autumn.

Today, as we witness an ever-accelerating fusion of peoples and cultures, and as intellectual exchanges multiply, a national art makes no sense. Thus the artificial effort by the Mexican painters to make one was foredoomed by its very anachronism. Taking some features of past cultures and mixing them with some modern art does not create a "national art." In those countries of the old continent where such an art exists, or did exist, it resulted from the slow differentiation of peoples over millennia; it was never invented full-fledged by intellectuals in the grips of nationalism. Witness the abortive ventures in Brittany or Catalonia.

Yet one cannot deny that there is an exceedingly rich and brilliant Mexican art, not created by the artists now in vogue, but having welled up from the people; or rather, having survived and grown among people crushed beneath centuries of fierce colonization and barbaric religious oppression, and now menaced by American bad taste. This art, far from being created out of thin air, attests to the rich culture of pre-Colombian societies and the artistic vitality of the people. The great artist of old, who decorated the innumerable temples found throughout Mexico with sumptuous frescoes, survives through those who now create *ex-voto* pictures (*retablos*) and *pulqueriá* wall-paintings. An art is there in embryo; but it is not to be found in the large advertising billboards of Diego Rivera and others. One might go so far as to say that, among the Mexican people, the professional artists are the least artistic.

Indeed, the deep current of popular thought, the poetry of the Mexican people, is expressed today in the *pulqueriá.* Witchcraft, as we know, was pervasive in pre-Columbian Mexican society, and everything was an occasion for bewitchment and magic. Christianity, despite the brutality with which it was introduced and although it slowly drove out the ancient gods, was powerless to change radically the population's thinking—simply because the invading clergy brought a religion so full of degenerate witchcraft that within it the Indians had no trouble propitiating their ancestral gods. The *ex-votos* are the descendants of both the figurines that the Indians presented to their gods as homage or to earn appeasement, as well as the innumerable *tepi-toton,* or household gods, which adorned their homes.

The *pulqueriá* paintings emerge from the same social and historical context as *pulque,* or fermented *agave* juice. Low in alcoholic content but nevertheless highly potent, *pulque* was the sacred drink in the Central Mexican plateau, from whence, through the Spanish conquest, it gradually spread to the entirety of the Aztec-dominated territory. Its invention seems to date from the period of the Toltec Empire. This Empire was destroyed by barbarians from the North sometime between the eleventh and twelfth centuries. Apparently, during this time, *pulque* enjoyed supernatural protection from the "400 rabbits." It is uncertain whether these were 400 distinct gods or a single deity with that name. 400 is the square of 20, a number that is sacred in the vigesimal system of the Nahua (along with 4 and 13), and that signifies metaphorically that which is innumerable.[1] In conjunction with the 400 rabbits, there were other *pulque* deities, the names and characteristics of which varied from one tribe to another, just as the legends concerning the invention of *pulque* varied from tribe to tribe. *Pulque* making was regulated by very strict rituals, and until recently it was the only drink of the Mexican people.

The mythical origins of *pulque*, and its primitive sacredness, reverberate today in the many poetic synonyms for it that can be found in the vernacular and on the signs of the places where it is drunk, the *pulquerías*. These, together with the names of buses and trucks, convey the genius of the Mexican people, and reveal their poetry and sense of humor. Here are a few taken at random: *La Linea de Fuego* (The Line of Fire); *Aqui me Quedo* (Here I Stay); *La Lucha por la Vida* (The Struggle for Life)— hundreds of similar expressions can be found. *El Tigre del Pedregal* (The Pedregal Tiger) refers to an animal said to have escaped from the zoo and terrified the inhabitants of the Pedregal lava flow, which stretches from the volcano Ixtle to the gates of Mexico City. *Las Mulas de Don Cristocal* (Don Christopher's Mules) refers to an amusing story. This *pulquería* was originally "The Knights of Columbus," but the church took this as an insult to the Catholic society of that name (of which the author had probably never heard) and pressured the police to force him to alter the sign. To vent his feelings about the clergy, all he could think to write was "Don Christopher's Mules." Mule in the popular language means something like "idiot." In addition to signs that refer to anecdotes, we find signs whose poetry is utterly gratuitous—such as that on a *pulquería* front as you enter San Bartolo Naucalpan: *Chifla el Mono* (Madden the Monkey); or one in Pachuca: *El Viento de la Cabeza* (The Wind of the Head); or again in Puebla: *El Hueso* (The Bone) which is equivalent to the French expression *l'assiette au beurre* ("soft job," "hit the jackpot"); and finally *El Recuerdo de Porvenir* (The Remembrance of things to Come) which was originally a sign on an undertaker's establishment. The next tenant, upon opening his tavern, did not deem it necessary to change the sign that had come with the premises.

One can hardly fail to see the link between these *pulquería* names and those of the buses and trucks where the humorous inspiration is often more direct. I remember an old truck panting up a steep hill with the melancholic motto on its rear: *Se sufre, joven!,* (One suffers, young man!). More often, pretentious claims can be read that are far from justified by the condition of the vehicle: *Allá nos vemos* (We'll meet down there), implying a velocity the truck is incapable of. Sometimes there are ironic inscriptions: one refers to President Truman's trip to Mexico on the "Sacred Cow," whence *El Chico Sagrado* (The Sacred Goat), except that in the vernacular *chico* means something between a rascal and a police spy. Here, then, humor prevails.

The inherent artistic feelings of the Mexicans express themselves in a thousand ways. A single market, no matter how poor, will convince anyone of this. Here, an Indian woman in rags wears dazzling colored wools braided into her black hair, and offers for sale little mounds of fruit built into pyramids at regular intervals. Elsewhere, baskets with a great variety of forms and colors are displayed. Further on, a potter unpacks his wares with their sentimental inscriptions. Popular art breaks through everywhere; even the poorest houses in the most miserable neighborhoods of Mexico City are decorated with flowers, as they were in the time of the Conquest, when art was under the protection of several deities. The gods are dead, including those of the Christians, but the art has remained. It has journeyed underground. It lives humbly on in the Indian *choza*, having persisted through all the tyrannies, exactions and cruelties. The Mexican people live in conditions so precarious as to be inconceivable in Europe (except perhaps in Russia), and attach themselves to even the slightest aesthetic detail that promises to adorn a miserable existence.

The persistence of art among the Mexican people can be attributed above all to the Indians' largely passive resistance to their oppressors—a resistance that, despite its general passivity, sporadically broke out in unbelievably violent explosions. The Indian people contrived to find leisure even if this meant sacrificing the indispensable. The concept of the "starving artist"—a concept that lives on amongst us, albeit often in a clichéd or stereotyped form—conveys a similar reality. Like the Mexican popular artist, the "starving artist" sacrifices the useful to the agreeable and reduces his material needs to the most elementary. This does not mean that the "starving artist" is always satisfied— far from it. In fact, there is no art without leisure. The United States, intent on immediate profit and absorbed in frenzied material activity, lacks art in the same way that a lizard lacks feathers. Here, humans have no time to be artists. In France, the conditions of modern life have caused popular art to disappear almost completely; the collective expression of art has given way to individual creation, with all the attendant vices of commercialism, hucksterism, etc. In Mexico, art, though no longer collective, has remained largely anonymous. The artist is first of all an artisan, and it is as inconceivable for such an individual to sign a *pulqueriá* painting as to sign a chair. The trademark was characteristic of periods of decline in the ancient world, as it is today; and advertising is something undreamed of by the folk artist.

The *pulqueriá* paintings represent the raw art of popular consciousness; they reveal peoples' consciousness just as spirals of smoke announce the volcano that tomorrow will spurt its streams of fire. Art enables communication between the artist and his public. It puts both the artist and the public on the same plane, allowing them to share desires, each expressing the aspirations of the other. These conditions are fully realized in the *pulqueriá* paintings, which fully partake in the material life and spiritual being of the people. They reflect the whole universe of Mexico's disinherited strata, from *agave* to cock-fighting, with its tremendous sorrows and its momentary joys. You need only walk by a *pulqueriá* and hear the uproar of songs, guitars, and shouts—sometimes, alas, punctuated by a pistol shot—to understand the role that this place, and hence its décor, plays in the life of the Mexican people. It is the very axis of their existence, their hope and consolation. We can hardly be surprised that they want to keep it beautiful. In a perfectly authentic way, the *pulqueriá* represents the universal desire for beauty disengaged from any kind of utility.

Translated by Mary Low

Notes

1. Compare with the meaning of the French expression: "*faire les 400 coups*" ("sow your wild oats;" "cut loose").

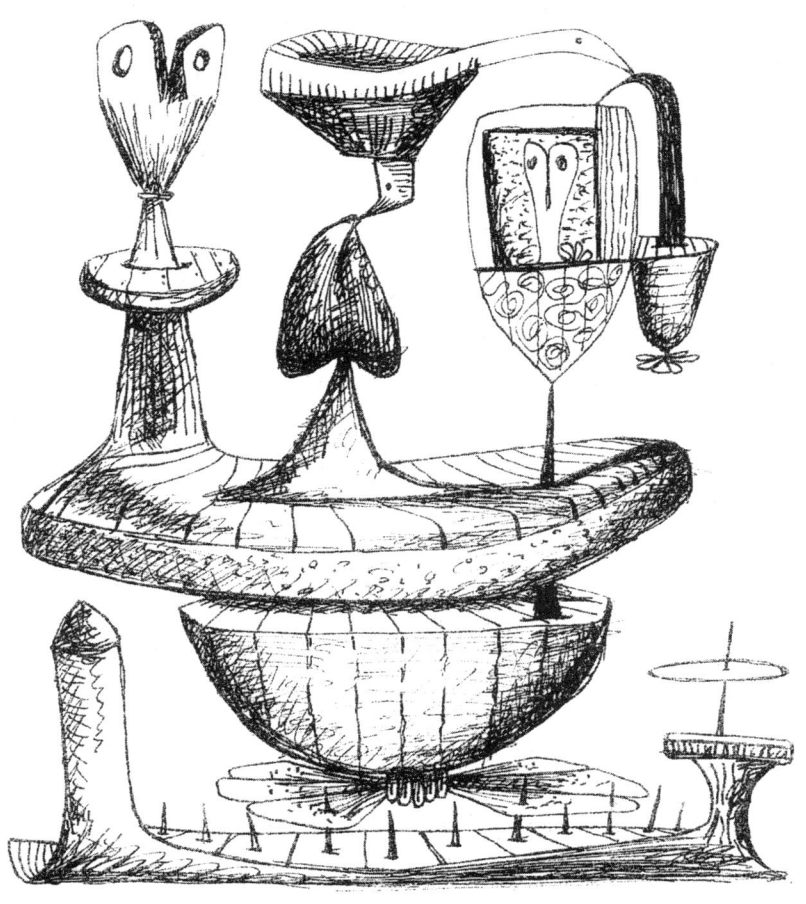

Eugenio F. Granell: Monument for a Gardener, 1953

LA PAROLE
est à
PÉRET

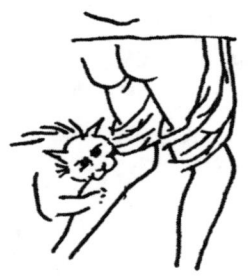

EDITIONS SURREALISTES

1 9 4 3

Title page of *La Parole est a Péret* (Péret has the Floor)

THOUGHT IS *ONE* AND INDIVISIBLE
Conscious and Unconscious Thought

I S IT BY CHANCE that the 18th century in France, the century of the "philosophy of enlightenment," did not produce any poets except the Marquis de Sade, who—despite his participation in the events of this epoch—expressed the first violent protest against the essential postulates of this period?

Let us admit right away that the "philosophy of enlightenment" was bragging without cause, since it merely replaced a foggy twilight with the first glimmers of a still foggy dawn. Its sole but essential merit was that it overthrew religion, as well as the entire philosophy and social structure that religion had engendered. But, in throwing God down the drain, it did not (or could not) destroy the material conditions that had produced him and that ultimately enabled a lay divinity to fill the breach left by his death. The "philosophy of enlightenment" attempted, upon destroying religion, to install reason—which had become the standard of all thought—in the niche that had been vacated by religion. If, hitherto, reason was a function of divinity and was therefore tolerated only insofar as it tended to justify and reinforce the celestial revelation, the position was now simply reversed, with a victorious reason rejecting everything that fell outside its field of vision.

The progress achieved, although it was immense because it involved the elimination of God, the obstacle to all knowledge, remained nevertheless precarious because, in place of a divinity that had become celestial, an earthly divinity was raised. Reason, like all divinities, soon started trying to climb surreptitiously into heaven so as to dominate the world. In political terms, it was not a revolution on the philosophic scale but a pronunciamiento, a coup d'etat, which preserved for the new master the benefits that the previous one had appropriated, with the caveat that the upstart, having revealed the path of revolt and having sought to elucidate the origins of revolt, became by this fact a more vulnerable tyrant than its predecessor.

Poetry is the source and the crown of all thought. Thus, the concept of Reason that was produced by the "philosophy of enlightenment" is, like the divinity it succeeded, nothing but a monstrous product of poetry, ashamed of its disavowed origin. In the midst of the battle between the monsters of God and Reason, poetry could not help but receive the blows. People attempted to imprison it in the narrow cell that the new God reserved for all that extended beyond its immediate field of activity, but it slipped through their fingers, and they were only able to retain its cast-off clothing. Poetry was elsewhere, feverishly wielding the indispensable guillotine. The only poetry of the 18th century that exalted the universe was the collective and grandiose French Revolution, which nevertheless was armed intellectually only with the very Reason that had been turned into poetry's enemy.

Despite this, the revolutionaries did not lack faith in poetry; on the contrary, they rendered absolute homage to it. It is true that during this epoch poetry was little more than a *zombie*, a well-powdered half-wit. The marvelous, the heart and nervous system of all poetry, having been thoughtlessly relegated to the same cupboard as religious superstition, was not given free-reign in the new-born rationalist thought—a thought that expressed itself, at least in the poetic domain, with a dry rhetoric, a kind of cuttle bone on which the canaries emulously sharpened their beaks so as to better give voice to their victorious trills. The marvelous is in any case no better off today; it remains the enemy because reason has not yet been hurled down from its celestial throne. Even Freud, in the final pages of *The Psycopathology of*

Everyday Life, feels the need to oppose himself to the marvelous. Of course this is a vain precaution: the marvelous gushes forth like an artesian well between each line of his book.

Ever since the 18th century, a veiled struggle between reason and poetry has been waged. Certainly, poetry appears to remain above the fray. The high artistic and cultural value of poetry is still recognized, but only that poetry which possesses nothing but the name, a situation that allows authentic poetry to be attacked all the more easily. And what is worse, there is not a single bandit of commerce or the church who does not feel himself possessed by the passion of poetry right up till the time he takes his first trip to the brothel. Apart from this meager existence, poetry's arms and legs are chopped off in an implacable war of drawn knives. Reason demands that thought be served in neat slices—beefsteaks of thought neatly and easily measured, assessable in money, exchangeable in motorcars, women, jewels. Why, it is asked, should this world have a need of poetry? It has money, and all that is not directly or indirectly translatable into monetary terms remains without value in the eyes of the Reason, because such things cannot augment the material wealth of the world.

In the United States, when people evaluate their monthly or yearly wages, they are accustomed to say "everything has its price." Even if such a process of evaluation is utterly contemptible, it has at least the faint merit of a revolting cynicism which is, on the whole, preferable to the general hypocrisy which consists in condemning verbally the monetary scale of values while referring to it surreptitiously at the same time. It follows that such a world only needs a poetry that flatters and amuses it, that lulls it to sleep so as to ease its sluggish digestions, and not a poetry that would awaken it and disturb it, guiding it toward truly creative, and consequently subversive, action. Poetic intuition remains, then—through its disruptive character—the fatal enemy, because it dares to conjure forth what it is better not to see: this world's future. Whence the discredit under which it vegetates in its most audacious guise: prophetic intuition. In contrast, hypothesis—reason's daily adventure, impure prophecy which is ashamed of its name—enjoys a favor that is ever more inordinate and ever less justified. For if one were actually to take account of the vast quantity of "scientific" hypotheses put forward, and the ridiculously small number of those that remain accurate today (only to be invalidated tomorrow), one would agree that there is little promise in "hypothesis" with which one might rally the prophets. On the contrary, it is very probable that the proportion of error is less great among the latter than among the blind followers of rationalist thought.

Whenever a minor or insignificant event of the previous day sets a dream in motion or enters into it, whether symbolically or not, this event is transformed by the dream, it assumes an astonishing significance therein. The dream seems to be so insignificant that it requires a whole process of dream analysis to uncover it—a penny doll—from beneath the crumbled day's debris.

I am convinced that one should see in dreams a sign of protest by the unconscious against the restraint imposed on it by the conscious mind; dreams constitute an effort to shake off the restraints engendered by society and by the education that society dispenses—an education that is nothing less than a drill inflicted on society's members, from childhood on. The values of conscious reality, perceived across the deforming prison of rationalist education, are thus completely overthrown since the insignificant becomes the essential. A new scale of values is created, having nothing in common with that which ruled us in our previous state. Which of the two is true, which is real and de-

serves to serve as our guide? To my mind, both of them are taint-
ed with faults that render them difficult to utilize.

The scale of values perceived by the conscious mind is the
rational product of absurd and loathsome social constraints; but
the scale suggested by the unconscious, on which the repressive
force of the conscious mind weighs, is without doubt equally
systematized, and its violently protesting character renders it del-
icate and difficult to use. In fact, we find ourselves in the pres-
ence of two foreign and hostile worlds, acting and reacting on
one another; the world of the conscious mind tyrannizes the
world of the unconscious, within which the profoundest human
aspirations are compressed. The latter reacts and rebels increas-
ingly against the oppression it suffers, and charts a line of con-
duct hostile to its adversary. If the crisis becomes acute, if all un-
derstanding is made impossible by the brutal eruption of the un-
conscious into the conscious, then, as one knows, the whole train
of neuroses, obsessions, phobias, etc. appears.

The proliferation of these troubles throughout the civilized
countries at the present time shows that the discord between
these two worlds has become generalized; the multiplication of
these extreme cases is indicative of a latent disturbance among
all individuals. The society that governs the conscious mind is
badly constructed, as this general discord proves. In the human
house a tacit agreement must be established between the two ten-
ants—conscious and unconscious—based upon mutual conces-
sions, because if the one continues to close the door when the
other wishes to leave, the latter will inevitably avenge itself one
day by setting the house on fire.

This potential agreement would always remain unstable be-
cause even though the conscious mind is disposed to put up with
everything and tries dictatorially to force the unconscious into
the same pliability, the latter remains the eternal rebel: pre-emi-

nently nonconformist, it is ready to revolt at the first occasion that arises, following the transformation of present society.

What then is the use of this revolution, since the conflict will be reborn—this conflict which forms a part of man so markedly as to constitute a permanent characteristic? There is no question at all of suppressing it, for that would be to suppress the source of all knowledge and creation; rather one should take notice of it and understand the terms of the dispute so as to enable consciousness, always moving and renewing itself, to bring about a solution. The concessions should always come from the conscious mind rather than the unconscious—that cosmic individual in whom desire, the sovereign phoenix which engenders itself indefinitely from its own ashes, resides—because, being the social individual, the conscious mind is always wrong form the viewpoint of human necessities and destiny.

The phenomenon of second-sight clearly obeys the same laws as does the dream. Its images are like those of the premonitory dream, insignificant both with regard to the conscious scale of values and in relation to the general picture from which they are detached. This is without any doubt due to the fact that the seer has, without realizing it and automatically, established a minimum harmony between his unconscious and his conscious, allowing the former comparative liberty. Instead of curbing it, he lets the reins slacken on the withers.

The operation does not, of course, succeed every time, because it presupposes a state of receptivity that is excessively unstable, this receptivity being more or less stimulated according to the physical and mental dispositions of the seer and remaining sometimes deaf to all stimulation. Likewise, all dreams are not obviously premonitory, although this point appears to me to be a ground for important queries. In fact, what passes for a premonitory dream in our eyes is nothing else than a dream in which a premonition leaps out to even the blindest eyes; but nothing hitherto proves that the Freudian interpretation of dreams is the only possible and valid one—nothing prevents us from supposing that oneiric symbols may be susceptible to an augural interpretation in numerous cases, if not always. In fact, in dreams the control by the conscious mind is probably even less rigid than with the seer, in whom it seems to be reduced to the minimum compatible with social life. What does it matter if I seem to want to rehabilitate the "Key to Dreams?" Freud, who cannot be suspected of making concessions to "superstition," freely acknowledges having derived some valuable instruction from it.

If prophetic texts, properly so called, do not ordinarily meet with anything but incredulity and condescending smiles on the part of the reader, it is astounding to observe with what ingenuity and constancy this same reader allows himself to be misled by his newspapers' predictions concerning the organization of the world after the war—by the same newspapers which had declared that the 1914 war would be the last, that the prosperity was assured for eternity, the present-day conflict was impossible, etc. From whence then comes this confidence, this blind faith which has everything in common with the religious faith from which it derives, in the charlatans who have no other aim but to deceive the reader? And from whence comes this distrust of prophets and seers? One must above all consider this attitude as resulting from rationalist education which, in most cases, assigns to intuition merely the status of the porter, whereas, in reality, it is the engineer in charge of operations, the only savant, the great inventor, the creator of reason itself.

Like Hitler or Stalin who were raised to power by the deluded masses and then promptly turned around and oppressed the masses, reason, in the realm of the spirit, crushes intuition with the power it has usurped from intuition. Rationalism, the intel-

31

lectual weapon of the bourgeoisie in revolt against the feudal system and its religion, springs to life in the 18th century and triumphs with the French Revolution. It was only to be expected that, since the feudal system had been eliminated in the name of reason, this same reason should become the supreme spiritual measure; because for the new masters, arrogant with their triumphs, it was the same spirit that had conquered "superstition." Superstition was understood at that time, as it is today, as everything that bordered on science, that is to say, everything that escaped the precise standard.

The precise standard of the epoch that commenced with the French Revolution and that, to our misfortune, is still the epoch in which we live today, is money. Aided by the tolerance engendered by common interests, it has practically ceased to be such, and remains merely a rival against which the struggle continues, without, however, preventing bargains behind the scenes. The enemy today, as always, is intuition, which first incurred the enmity of religion and then created reason, which is just as hostile to it, although reason destroys the comforting legend in order to restore everything to the world of man. But first of all one must learn to know man. It is not enough to direct him like a robot in the name of an omnipotent reason, to send him to get himself killed on the battlefields in the name of liberty, to make him toil like a beast of burden in the name of an equality which produces the shareholder and the worker, to imprison him for all and for nothing in the name of a fraternity which produces the jailer and the prisoner.

Insofar as one has not achieved an insight into the determining role of intuition, one will continue to remain on the level of the priest preaching a religion, be it a traditional religion or the lay religion of reason. Reason, denying religion but allowing those material conditions that enabled the creation of religion to subsist, could not fail to inherit many corruptions from its prede-cessor, just as the son inherits certain positive qualities from his parents.

It rests with our epoch, which already has as its responsi-bility the material transformation of the world, to abolish all gods including reason and to restore man to man. "The world of man is man" (Karl Marx), without god or reason to rule him, or to prevent him, as André Breton has put it, from "becoming aware of himself contradictorily," from understanding that there is no thought without intuition—that is to say without second-sight—and no intuition without thought.

Translated by Mary Low

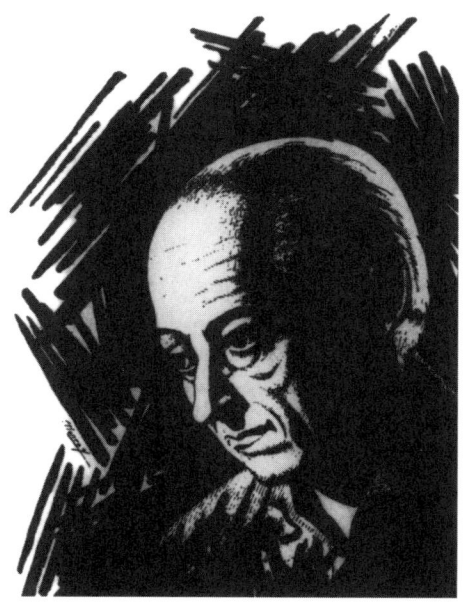

Portrait of Péret by Man Ray

AUTOMATIC WRITING

W HO, AMONG ALL the readers of this journal, has not been struck by the strange poetry of his dreams? Who has not lived, during his sleep, one or several vibrant, tormented lives, far more real and captivating than his wretched daily life? Before sleeping and dreaming, have you never been astonished, while you were steeped in some kind of somnolence, at the ideas, the images, the phrases that came into your mind and revealed to you worries that you were not aware of in your wakeful state? You have been, moreover, able to ascertain that the same phenomenon occurred as soon as you let your mind wander at random. That is because there, conscience is abolished, or nearly so. Reason has retired to its kennel and is chewing its eternal bone.

All you need, then, is to drive away this reason-bitch and write, write without stopping, without considering the tumult of your ideas. There is no further need to know what an alexandrine or a litotes is. Take a hand, paper, ink, and a pen with a new nib, and settle yourself comfortably at your table. Now forget all your worries, forget that you are married, that your child has whooping-cough, forget that you are Catholic, that you are a senator, that you are a disciple of Auguste Comte or of Schopenhauer, forget antiquity, the literature of all countries at all times. You no longer want to know what is logical and what is not, you no longer want to know anything except what you are going to be told. Write as fast as possible so as not to lose any of the secrets that are made known to you about yourself, and above all do not re-read yourself. You will soon notice that, little by little as you write, the sentences become faster, stronger, more alive. And if, by chance, you find that you stop suddenly, don't hesitate, force the door of the unconscious and write the first letter of the alphabet, for example. The letter A is as good as any other. Ariadne's thread will return by itself. Having said that, I begin.

A bunch of asparagus that is not quite seven leagues long is exhausting itself cutting out a rainbow in a box of shoe polish. The rainbow runs along the beach looking for a pipe made of foam. It hears the sea in the hollow of its hand and becomes, after thirty years of study on an island of shifting sands, a ship's captain. It is then that the king of a commonplace country gives him a soup tureen as a present. He puts some tortoise eggs in it, and when the moon changes the soup tureen flies off like the last sigh of a consumptive. Yet it was a very beautiful night and the stars, after having lost at baccarat, had gone off to fish for trout with cars' headlights.

Everything would have been perfectly alright if the grand duchess Anastasia had not that very day eaten a large page of emery paper. In no time, the grand duchess, having taken over the bank, lost her head. The rest of her body followed rapidly and soon there was nothing left but her toe-nails that went off to draw a lighted billboard in a dark corner full of noises of jaws opening and closing following the rhythm of "au clair de la lune, mon ami Pierrot…" There was nothing for the distressed spectator of this scene to do but swallow a very large cup of black ink. He did so without too much repugnance, even though the very high temperature would have made pens grow in his ink. After that he closed the shutter of his window and fell asleep, and fell asleep like a saucer that someone has forgotten to top with a coffee-cup. But if the coffee pours in a shower down the sleeper's neck, he is of course obliged to yell fire in order to call the firemen. They arrive like salted herrings and here they are with their weapons on their shoulders, no longer knowing where the barrels of their rifles are, putting cartridges up their noses, pulling the janitor's ear, eating the parrot's seeds, putting leeches in the manager's shoe-box, eating mosquito fries and pulling the devil by the tail so as to be led quickly and at small expense to their grandmothers. The poor old lady is nothing but skin and bones. From time to time she sells a bit of her skin to make a drum which she sends to one of her grandsons on his birthday. It is rather touching, but a little silly, because when she has been reduced to a skeleton state she will not have resources to live in haunted houses, since her landlord hates the noise of bones on the stairs which are already quite worm-eaten.

Time goes by and the Earth turns, flies fly, water flows under bridges that have not known what to do with their arches since the death of Noah, who is so dead that the lice that nested in his ear have taken refuge on dogs, on dogs that give their hair to cats at cockcrow. The source of the beet might well dry up and saltpeter cover the pope's nose before the acanthus leaves take the bit between their teeth. This is not so with ladybugs, which authority has put into straitjackets in contempt of all justice. But justice only wears old heelless shoes through stinginess and her scales have weighed so many rotten potatoes that they tell the time like an old cuckoo. Cuckoo! Cuckoo! That's him, the little soldier with frozen feet. He goes "one….two…." and there he goes rolling to the foot of the stairs and drives his head into the letter-box. One more pane broken, but the glazier won't be able to do anything about it because he is, at the moment, very busy cutting out some pants for himself from an old factory chimney.

His own flew away on the 14th of July. They took themselves for a captive balloon and wanted to get free. They even succeeded. I wish them good luck. The glazier, their owner, wasn't interesting. He had rye bread eyes and he used to moo on Sundays, watching the bicycles go by, which wasn't proper. Sometimes the bicycles took revenge and from their free wheel, threw flint-stones at him. As he had no rifle, he cooked the stones with floating-laundry jam. That's how he thought about opening a restaurant and made his fortune. Now he is a minister of finance and rich as hot sauce. He dresses in all kinds of herbs, good and bad, which has earned him the blessings of the vines and vine-growers. Wine is neither better nor worse for it, but the wine-growers are drunker than ever.

One sees them everywhere, even on the roofs of houses where, in their instants of lucidity they replace the tiles and expedite the discharge of rainwater which they swallow unhesitatingly. Whatever the weather may be, they stroll around and sharpen their teeth on their daggers or vice versa. Their teeth are their tools, whether it is a matter of eating apples or killing time. And their pursed lips swallow the four-leaf clovers' day, but luck is relative and a four-leaf clover does not always protect itself from a wall-flower that has five, like potpourri covering a yellow cat. If he is yellow it is because he has been roasted and the clover's four leaves multiplied by the wall-flower's five can do nothing about it. That's the trouble. He has a fork in his left hand and a pair of pincers in his right hand. In the twinkling of an eye, he tears the nose off the bold ones, takes it with his fork and puts it down at the poste restante. As for the nose, it doesn't worry about such little things. It knows its turn will come and it will be able to revenge itself like cherries ripen; but in the meanwhile it will have to take care and pull out, little by little, the long hairs which try to re-cover it. Otherwise the local toupee-maker will take it for a wig and put it on the skull of his bald wife.

Translated by Mary Low

WIFREDO LAM

THE TRUE MISSION of the artist—painter or poet—has always been to find within himself the archetypes underlying poetic thought, to charge them with a new affectivity, so that an energetic current may circulate between himself and his fellow men, all the more intense in that these actualized archetypes will appear as the clearest and freshest expressions of the atmosphere that has conditioned the artist. It is easy to discern this process at work in those poetic or plastic works that have had the most lasting influence. For example, Ubu can quite legitimately claim a certain kinship with Cronos. In renewing the latter, Jarry has at the same time announced the reincarnation of Ubu in the modern world. And one knows that his prophecy continues to be fulfilled every day.

Has Wifredo Lam, taking as his point of departure the beliefs of West Indian black people, voluntarily embarked on a similar course? It is doubtless too early for us to discern, within his work, that which expresses the essential element of man, as this might be defined by common agreement between the African sorcerer and the Asian shaman—two types of people who fortuitously fuse within him and thus persist. We can see that Lam has managed to penetrate the cavern within which, throughout all eternity, dragons and angels do battle without mercy, linking together and transforming themselves. Like his ancestors, Lam seizes the "spirits" at their source in an attempt to grasp their matter, forces them to reveal their secret, and does not free them into sheaves of black flames and cries of passion until they submit to his desires. Lam's heritage—one that involves racial hybridity—can be discerned in his canvases. This heritage is taken up by him as subject matter, and is subjected to a chain of metamorphoses whose end, if it exists, remains invisible to him. To tell the truth, it is not "Nago" or "Bambara" divinities that vitalize the beings of his imagination, just as these beings do not reign over West Indian hearts: they have known too many vicissitudes and suffered too many embraces. But these beings, real tiger cubs, serve to express that eternal depth of the spirit which, in every language and in every tone, speaks alternatively of desire and terror. These states of being, which Lam transfigures in order to resolve their opposition on a higher plane, drawing them into a continuous upward movement, are those which all men have known and still know. Only the images that they engender are different today from what they were yesterday, different here from what they are there, not only in their contents but in their aspect, just as a blackbird reveals its place of origin by its plumage. But Lam, by seizing them at their point of creation, has been able to impart to these images the brilliance of both paradise and hell, showing that they are intermingled with one another. For this reason, his work simultaneously bewitches and enchants.

In calling such beings to life, Lam does not mean to cover them with new tinsels, but on the contrary to tear away from each one whatever might conceal its real nature. It is the tropical forest—now howling, now haunted by the menacing silence of deserts—in which these faces loom up, rendered furious by the tom-tom-like sound of water dripping on leaves that are always green. In truth, this grin is only a flower gleaming in the dusk, like the eye of a watchful animal. And if by chance a ray of sunlight glimmers among the fallen trunks, it surely means in doing so to point out a scarlet bird busily smoothing its feathers. Nothing, apparently, that does not belong everywhere! And yet nothing is found elsewhere, for the tension that reigns here is unique and permanent. It is that of the prairie Indian on the warpath, attentive to the smallest sign given by the ground on which he treads. It is also that which Lam brings to his paintings, which seem to result from a prodigious accumulation of power freed in blinding flashes of lightning. Here, nothing lets go. In the underworld that he explores, the event expected from one second to another is just as likely to be favorable as baneful. Regardless, it has for us all the traits of the marvelous, multiplying itself to infinity by its own accord. Nobody will therefore be surprised at this tension which is sometimes almost hostile, for Lam wanders at random in these buried forests that seem more virgin the more one wants to rape them, where the animals of times past continue to growl in every clearing. He is devoted to capturing them, not in order to tame them, but to show them to us in their savage state and in all their captivating fury, so that we may recognize them in ourselves.

Translated by Mary Low

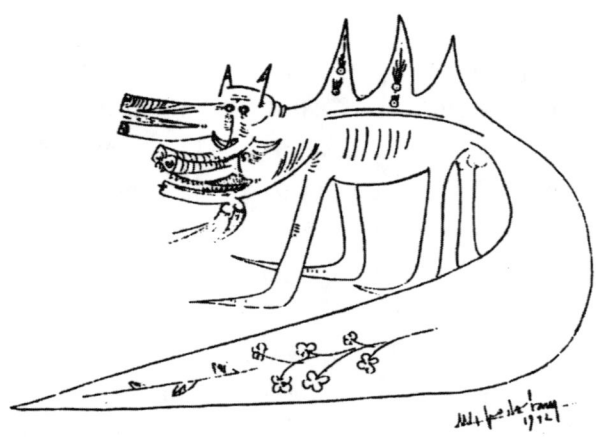

Wifredo Lam: Drawing from the cover of Amié Césaires'
***Return to My Native Land* which had a Preface by Péret**

PREFACE

to Aimé Césaire's Return to My Native Land

I HAVE THE HONOR of greeting here a great poet, the only great Francophone poet to appear in the last twenty years. For the first time a tropical voice rings out in our language, not in order to season an exotic poetry—the tacky decoration of a mediocre dwelling—but to expose the sparkle of a real poetry, springing from the rotted trunks of orchids and from electric, carrion-devouring butterflies; this poetry is a savage cry that rings out across an overbearing, sadistic countryside—a countryside that degrades men and their machines as flowers do rash insects.

Aimé Césaire owes nothing to anyone: his language—not merely his own—is the resplendent language of hummingbird arrows feeding in a mercury sky. Césaire, rather than simply being an interpreter of the tropical nature of Martinique, is also a part of it; he is a judge and an element of that nature at one and the same time. His poetry has the sovereign movement of the great breadfruit trees and the obsessive accent of vodun drumming. Black magic, pregnant with poetry, resists the pro-slavery religions, in which all magic is modified and in which all poetry lies dead for all time.

I have the honor of greeting here the first great black poet who has broken his mooring-lines and launched himself forth, without worrying about any pole star, any intellectual Southern Cross—guided solely by his blind desire.

It is wonderful, it greatly enthuses and comforts me, that in this year of 1942, (yet another year of misery and abjection), when all the poets and artists of Europe are suffocating, asphyxiated under mustaches—under the white mustache of Vichy that knows so well how to polish boots; the bullet-hole mustache of Berchtesgadem, etc.—a poet makes his unique cry heard from America, puncturing the opacity of this night of bombs and execution squads.

I have the honor…

Translated by Mary Low

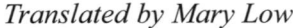

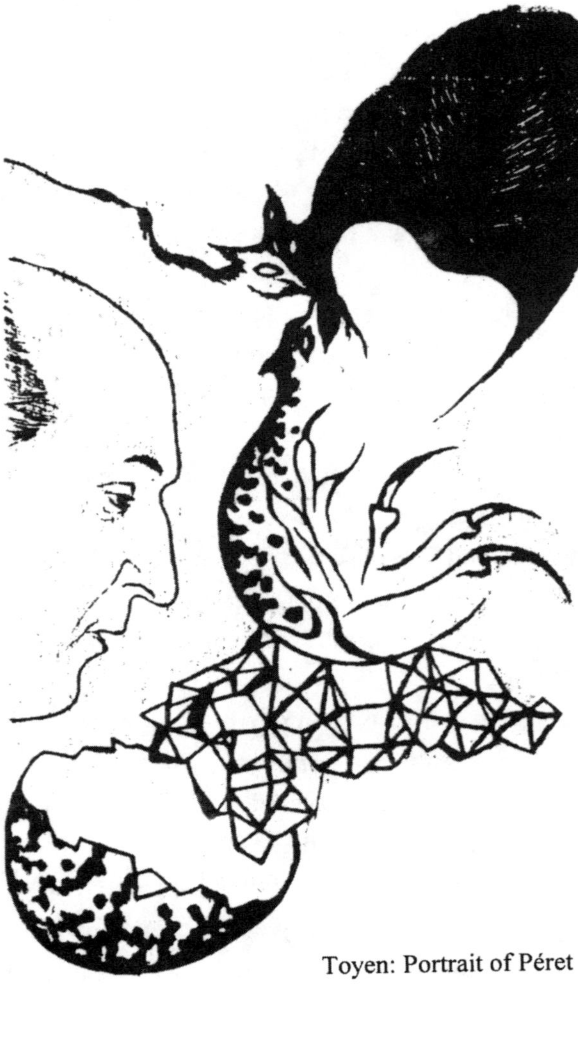

Toyen: Portrait of Péret

THE NEW WORLD FOUNDED BY TOYEN

J UST AS THE LEAF turns into a wing, an insect, a mushroom, a plate; just as the full-blown bean is borne away on a hesitant wing, Toyen makes the figure of a woman emerge gradually from an old wall, or conjures forth a wolf, gnawed by ox-tongues, from another wall. Toyen is never satisfied! For her, the world remains endlessly perfectible; the slightest jolt is enough to transform the world once more, just as it was transformed at the beginning of our era, when a semblance of order first began to emerge out of what had been merely a chaotic and antagonistic mass of elements. At this originary moment, nothing had yet acquired permanent form. A hen's egg was just as likely to give birth to a monkey as to an agate. Everything was at the mercy of everything else, not only in matters of life and death, but also with respect to the inscrutable future. This formative moment seems to have passed.

However, Toyen suggests that, on the plane where the external world is merely one element in the composition of a complete world, we can, if we wish, re-live this moment ourselves from day to day: the perception of a bird's song may provoke the resurrection of cities long since submerged, or your next door neighbor may ride a bicycle at the head of a procession of giraffes, chanting hymns of praise to the sun.

The sole purpose of Toyen's work is to reshape the external world in accordance with a desire that emerges all on its own, and that swells with its own fulfillment. During the period when she first began to yield to this desire (1927), her work depicted nothing but apparitions of this new world—or even merely sketchy outlines of apparitions; whereas now every picture Toyen paints represents a distinct phase of a continuous process of metamorphosis, and the entire corpus of her work depicts an entirely new world—a world wherein Toyen, conducting the orchestra of forms and colors, tones down a shade here, brightens one up there, shifts the emphasis round to the right, then to the left, bringing into strong relief a previously mundane detail.

At the precipice where our soil is already touched with light
Lower your second eyelid, for the earth will dazzle you
If you raise your head

I like to imagine that Apollinaire, when he wrote these lines, was projecting himself forward—beyond the era and the insignificant personage to which they were dedicated—to Toyen. Toyen's inner eye never flinches when it contemplates her inner world—her only sun—and she is unafraid as she passes the ground upon which the rainbow erects its triumphal arch; she is fashioned from the sounding flash of unseen birds' songs, scattered in the wake of the winds, sweeping across the deserts. Black is the face of her sun, its lights transferred to the earth; blue is the face it conceals. Her eyes have been fixed on the earth so long that they have seen the mountains rise, tremble with fear, and spit forth crystals of lava like a young Mexican volcano—a volcano that buries churches under its lava, leaving only the memory of a tower standing, solitary like a Christian phantom, overcome by the eternal sleep of death.

According to Toyen's clock—so weary that its hands have abandoned it, preferring to make love in their little alcove—it is always noon. But no flaming orb illuminates the skies; for here, beyond the bounds of time, noon shells the peas for the swallows who no longer act as harbingers of spring, for they have published their memoirs and, averse to an unreliable climate, fly neither high nor low, intent on fashioning new lips. And the barometer is always fixed at "fine and settled" so that the owls may fulfill their floral vow in peace, and offer themselves, a living sacrifice, to the love song that rises from the forest.

Nevertheless, Toyen stays here, guarding the dawn against the threat of war as she drifts away, pinning down the spectres, which she classifies by colour, size and sex so that everyone can recognize them and accept or reject them as he will. Even the sleeping girl comes from the depths of her dream to strike the tuning A for the high grass, which is crowned with butterflies who chant the praises of the unruffled morn. There is cause for neither tears nor laughter: tears and laughter, reconciled at last, have combined to raise the banner of combat and to cast themselves upon tables green with terror. The horizon dons its festive garb, puts on its sword, pins on its medals and—stomping its heels vigorously—dissolves into the all-encompassing light; while fright, out on the horizon, is condensed into snowy flakes of foam, clinging like a leech on the senses, lying like starch upon the dress. Lifted by the hot air that rises from the surface of the earth, she exposes the target that she had been concealing and points to the relentless fight that is being waged—from the egg to the roasting spit—by the fowl of the air: a veritable military force.

Still noon! But what is happening to the coffee? It has lost its wits, just as it has lost its way in the labyrinth of bones that is strewn through the streets of an island after a storm. Not a single Pharaoh dares rise from the Nile, for fear of the hour, which creeps through the woods, lies down darkly, flat on its face, and stretches out like a string of barges along a canal flanked by vigilant fishes, whose luminous skeleton meanders forward, tracing the line of the far bank. Far away—as far away as a bird's song —the widening strokes of a pendulum, having already swung for half of eternity, indicate by the swelling amplitude of their movement that long shadows are attempting to stifle it, to escape its relentless momentum. By and by, the pendulum will slip down to watch the procession of the three Wise Men (who have travelled for so long that the dust has had time to glitter and waltz in a sunbeam), only to return to its place, and take up again—for the remaining half of eternity—the serenity of its oscillations.

Still noon, no doubt about that! The napes of women with skillfully set hair rise up on the horizon. Tense and still, they watch its attempts to approach, ready to drive it back with a crack of the whip. O Eagle, clasp thy hands, humble thy pride and beg of the reindeer—whose flesh is so transparent that the growth of its bones can be seen—to restrain its ardor, lest the eastern horizon hurl itself on top of the western, crushing you in between. Will thine hands, too white against the blood-red hue of thine eyes, make the sign that twines and intertwines, the sign awaited by the sparrows, who are gathering their strength in preparation for a flight that is doomed to end in bands of smoke? And will those bands write, on the white page of the green sky, the words that every man, in the depths of his soul, is constantly looking for and would continue reading forever, even if nothing more were being written, even if the streets were transformed into a long celestial way, flanked by protective poplars, in such a way as to make of every encounter a prelude to love? It doesn't matter! The wind, if it enters the room, will drink from the cup that was unintentionally left there by the surf; it will raise the eye-lids that conceal a pair of haunted eyes, and lay bare an arm whose repose can never be disturbed, just as the fire that consumes the firebird can never be extinguished.

Elsewhere, the myth of light is told in the following manner: "In the beginning was the black-gold rain. The wings of birds were losing their feathers as they lapped their wings in the rainstorm; in winter they grew slimy, like toads; in spring they sang the song of day; and in autumn they were gathered in, and suddenly flew away, leaving the rain to dash itself down on the ground. All was black and white. Black, the morning, and white the noon, and each day ended in black rain. The span of man's life was half a day. The black men, born in the morning, died at noon; and the others, the white, expired under the evening rain. Life continued in this way until one day, a couple took shelter from the evening rain and survived. It was autumn. They saw the wings of the rain fold up and vanish behind a white hill. The rain had ceased, and they climbed the hill; but the wings were already crossing another hill, dazzlingly white, whiter than anything else they had ever seen. And, behind that second hill, they perceived something unknown, light as a first breath, soft as untroubled sleep. Drawing near, they saw the wings of the rain spread out on the earth in exhaustion, gleaming with astonishing, unfamiliar lights. The blue lights were swaying gently to and fro, striving to attract the attention of the greens as they leered at the yellows, glared at the reds, and spit at the orange in their fury; whilst the violets stood apart, gnawing their nails with rage. Dazzled, they gathered up as much of the wings as they could carry away, saying: "Light is born; let us hand it on to the men of the future." And they traveled across the world, taking the light with them.

For the rest, we can only put our trust in the becoming of freedom; therein lies the origin of truth.

Biographical Note by Péret

Toyen was born in Prague, Sunday at six o'clock in the evening, on September 21, 1902. Before the end of World War I, she had already participated in numerous activities that signaled the emergence of a new epoch of revolutionary activity and avant-garde artistic manifestations. This avant-garde uprising belonged to no sect, but was rather a movement formed by individuals as diverse as Franz Kafka and Jaroslav Hasek, the author of *The Good Soldier Schweik.*

The group Devetsil emerged out of this movement. It served as the foundation for all those activities that, in the third decade of the century, made Czechoslovakia the focal point of the artistic avant-garde—an avant-garde represented in France by Dada and Abstract Art, in Germany by Bauhaus, in Italy by Futurism, and in Russia by Meyerhold, Taïroff, Maïakovsky, Pasternak, and Eisenstein. Due to the international spirit fostered by Devetsil, the Czechoslovakian public was provided with numerous translations of French poets, such as Lautréamont, Rimbaud, Apollinaire, Jarry and others. The revue *Red,* published by Devetsil, printed essays by Karel Teige that focused on trends in modern architecture, film, theatre, and poetry. This review also served as the tribune for a new generation of Czech artists and poets. Two of Devetsil's most prominent painters, Toyen and Jindrich Styrsky, have followed parallel artistic paths over the course of their lives. Toyen made her first appearance in 1923, during the first exposition of Devetsil.

Translated by Mary Low

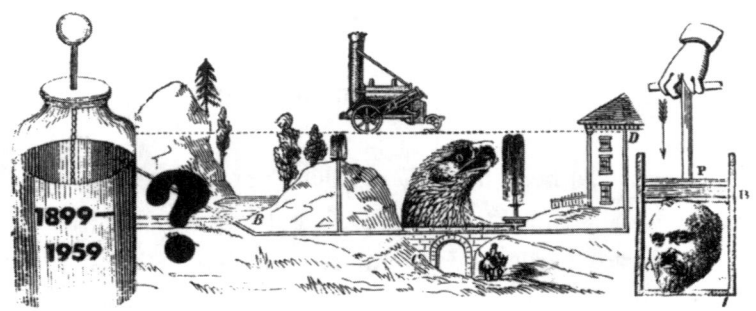

THE WORK OF JINDRICH STYRSKY

The right eye leads to the left eye which closes the circuit. Between them they register the painting of Jindřich Štyrský, permanent spark popping up between two threads attempting to meet. In vain one would search the drawings presented today for something other than the form of this spark and the world it illuminates, its own, where the mists of death hang around the cluster of eyes, cairns built to excite our wandering imagination. Nothing in Štyrský *is* but everything could *become* because his work places itself at the point where that wind is born which will fill the veils or ruffle the tiles of houses at the same time that it cries, here, soon will be floods, or there, plentiful harvests.

Each painting, each drawing by Štyrský throws the fire onto an intense second, charged with the paroxysm of a mass of obscure seconds. He doesn't carry on a love affair with the outside world but rather rapes it in broad daylight, obeying the imperious desire that flows from the depths of his being. If others transcribe, unbeknownst to them, the first successes of past ages, he restores to us the primordial bubbling of the species which creates myth. It's a cactus with scarlet flowers shooting up from a cold lava flow, an isolated statue that the harsh desert winds have exhumed from the sand, bearing witness to another epoch yet to be revealed.

One would search vainly in the oeuvre of Štyrský, whom death took from us in 1942, for one single concession to the current tastes or the pressures of the milieu. As a revolutionary, he rejected the tyranny of those false revolutionaries fierce to protect their obscurantism of rags which they think new, because, as a seeker, he fought against all constraints imposed in the name of interests pretending themselves to be superior. This pressing need for liberation pushed him through cubism and abstractionism in a whirlwind to finally recognize himself as a surrealist. Hitler's occupation of Czechoslovakia and the war were not able to divert him from his route, mixed with that of the revolution. All disinterested research serves, in effect, the cause of the emancipation of man; inversely, technical research is too often oriented to the fulfillment of the masters' needs and therefore opposed, at least in the current results, to the liberation of man whom we allege is now kept in eternal slavery.

***

At dawn, the voyager who exits the vast silent, dark forest discovers under his feet a burst agate. He looks at it and murmurs: "A solar eclipse!"

Translated by Madeleine Arenivar

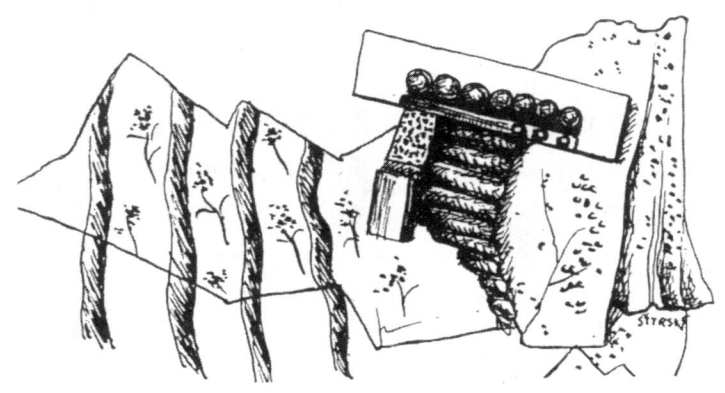

Štyrskỳ: Drawing

INSIDE THE ARMOR

W HEN HE HAD CAUGHT the fish that other animals ate, man thought of how to preserve it; he invented the can, modeled on the pelican's pouch. When he had launched his arrow like the bull launches its horns, man thought of how to protect himself from it; he invented armor, descendant of the turtle's shell, which arrows cannot penetrate.

There, back in the maternal womb, he defied the gods who fell on his head from the four corners of heaven: Germanic gods, Christian gods, Celtic gods, Moorish gods, to speak only of Europe. These gods, whom he had created from scratch by pouring nature out drop by drop, and to whom he had given permission to live bloody lives, turned against their creator who, trembling with awe, protected himself as best he could under the conscience of his breast-plate.

Dread wells up from the depths of man's being and shakes him like a bush of seaweed under a stormy sea. In vain does he stand up like a fallen rock in the middle of a field of oats; fear steals through the stems and gnaws at him until he topples over. Man falls, floundering in the murky darkness of Christianity. Touched, then jostled by savage shadows in which he recognizes all too clearly his own image (but nevertheless refuses to admit its intimate origin), he takes shelter behind a screen of mysticism, of ceremony, and shifts the weight of his own terror onto others.

Demons with cactus eyes threaten man at every turning of every path, in the creaking of every door, in the call of birds and in the rumble of torrents. To defend himself, he burrows down, mole-like, in the damp darkness of churches, where he thinks he will find shelter from himself, and hides inside armor in order to be better protected from outside attacks.

Imagination brings to light that which lies buried in the depths of man and of nature, insofar as nature itself is apprehended. Recognizing among his ancestors the great beasts of distant ages whose legends have come down to him, the medieval knight fashions his armor in their fabulous image, rebuilds the Trojan horse for his own purpose. He fights against other armors similar to his own, against himself. All these knights that have descended from the same distant ancestors, all these brother-enemies, can only be told apart thanks to their more recent forebears: the ermine, the falcon, the donkey, the eagle, as among the Indian tribes of North America and the Eskimos of today. The same totem pole that sits in the center of the Indian village shielded the heads of knights during the 14th and 15th centuries. It was outlawed as soon as its pagan origin was sensed, but took refuge in symbolic form, in the coats of arms created at that time.

Once his fear has passed, the knight in the shelter of his armor feels himself the equal of his fabled models, beings whose protection ensures his triumph. When he passes by, birds fly into the air, deer and wolves flee in terror, men, dominated, hide away.

With his lance at the ready, there is no earthly being that can resist him. He needs enemies equal to him, equal to the size of his giant shadow that cleaves the horizon. Now only the hydra and the dragon are worthy objects of his power. Only they can oppose him in combat. Only they can be conquered nobly. And if they steal away, he in his fury turns against the mountains, rending them with his sword.

The mystical dread that he felt up to then suddenly changes into a terror that rides at his side like an escort. The legend that gave his armor its terrifying outlines halos him in blood and lightning. He is the all-powerful master, the equal of the gods—gods who crumble at the slightest touch of his iron armor. Now a god, his only possible opponent is another god: that of the Moors, who sweep forward menacingly, mowing down the crucifixes with their crescent moon.

Sitting out in a twilight of blazing fields, the knight moves with a clinking of armor like the sound of coins on a marble slab. His lady companion, padlocked like a suburban villa, will soon be listening to tales of other armors, all the more astounding as they involve no convict's belt. The armory of battle becomes merely armor and combat becomes a sport where the knight is distinguished by his totem and followed from afar by the dame who sent him into battle.

Life reflected by the armor shines, iridescent, like a prism in the sun. And soon the belt, a tyrannical armor, will flee like a startled hare. Love emerges triumphant from the armor that stifled it. The victor of the tournament, lance held high, will enter as a willing prisoner into the glittering armor of love, which flashes like a meteor across a winter's night. Alas! He is engulfed by another armor which stealthily closes around him.

Let us open the armor. Let us open all the armors.

Translated by Alice Mayoux

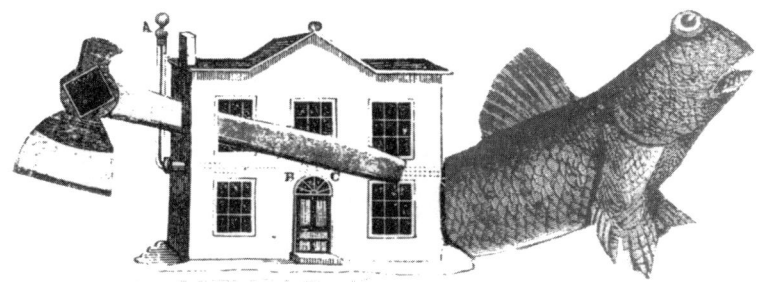

IN A CLINCH

TO WAKE UP IN the bottom of a carafe, stunned like a fly, is enough to make you kill your mother five minutes after you get out. That is what happened to me one morning, so it is not surprising that I now have a head like a dandelion and that my shoulders sag down to my knees. During the first few minutes after I woke up, I imagined that I had always lived in the bottom of a carafe and probably I would still believe it if I had not seen a sort of bird on the other side of the carafe, knocking it peevishly with his beak. Thanks to him, the accidental and annoying features of my situation were made clear to me and I flew into a rage. I seized a dry leaf which was near me and, shoving it into my left nostril, I cried: "Is it possible that the dog is a friend of man? Is it true the snail is the enemy of the turtle?" And from the top of the carafe, a fissure of glass murmured: "Poor idiot! Enemies are not as silly as people think. They have beards and their brains are made of celluloid scrapings and potato peelings. Friends have glass heads and bite like transmission belts."

But I insisted: "Is it true that flies do not die on clock hands? Is it true that rice straw is used to make meatballs? Is it true that oranges gush out of mine shafts? Is it true that bologna is made by blind people? Is it true that quails suck ewes? Is it true that noses get lost in fortresses? Is it true that bathrooms fade away into pianos? Is it true that the expression 'put out to grass' does not signify having frozen feet? Is it true that in dark rooms the song of dreams is never heard?"

He then made a great noise like a pot falling and rebounding on a stone staircase and a small opening appeared in my prison. Mercifully for me, it did not take long in growing to the

size of a railroad tunnel at the entrance of which appeared a
small creature which resembled both a sardine and a butterfly. I
was no longer alone and consequently I was in less of a hurry to
leave the carafe, which I began to find quite congenial. It would-
n't have taken much for me to have become inspired to ask the
sardine-butterfly to live with me, which probably she would not
have refused me, for she seemed very gentle and obliging. How-
ever, I did not risk making this proposition, which many would
have found strange, although it is no more extraordinary than
throwing a paving stone from a sixth storey window into a street
filled with a busy crowd in the hope of killing someone. But the
world is such that it is more scandalous to live with a sardine-
butterfly than to live alone in a carafe. And therefore I made no
proposal to this charming creature. In fact, in entering the carafe,
her wings folded beside her, her tail and fins disappeared, a spark
escaped from her head, followed by a small wisp of smoke, and I
saw nothing in its place but a signpost on which was written:
Scorpion, 200 KM 120.

Again I fell into a violent temper and grabbing the signpost
I threw it as hard as I could against my glass prison walls. To my
great astonishment the signpost went through the carafe and
bounced two or three times upon its outside surface before re-
ducing it to powder. It was then that I was surprised to find my-
self stretched out on my back in a field of wheat. As I made a
movement to get on my feet, twenty partridges flew out of my
pockets where they must have been hiding for a long time—al-
though I had not been aware of it—for they left a large number
of eggs that hatched in my hand.

Having recovered from my surprise, I reflected that one
field was as good as another. Not without difficulty, I succeeded
in regaining the vertical position for which I was born, and threw
jets of saliva to all sides, which flew with one hasty wing stroke,

followed by the shots of invisible hunters. I climbed into the ditch, taking care not to crush the pretty little white moles who were taking to the air and enjoying it naively. They could only enjoy this pleasure on rare occasions! They were so happy that, although I was a stranger to them, they could not restrain themselves from confiding their story to me. A very small white mole with dragon-fly wings told me the following tale:

Story of the White Mole

Just as you see me, I was born in a box of polish. My father was a chestnut vendor and my mother a sow. How did that happen? I cannot say. My father was a tall thin man, like a flint, except his head was as large as one can imagine. He had no nose and his ears hung like the stems of a creeping vine torn off by the wind. Naturally he was stupid, that is why he was a chestnut vendor. One day, having torn off a sow's tail, he walked throughout the city of Troyes shouting: this is my blood. Soon the druggists came after him, then the solicitors, hardwaremen, cesspool cleaners, lacemakers, orthopedists, justices of the peace, café keepers, sacristans, herb dealers, amateur fishermen, children of pigs, and finally the clergymen. Then, seized by an intense terror, he hid the sow's tail in a box of polish which he put in a letterbox with the following address:

    Clay Pipe
    at Ivory Tower
    near Scurvy (Morbihan)

And the letter went high and low. Soon it mounted an iceberg, then descended into a vat. Afterwards it climbed to the branch of a tree, the leaves of which it devoured. Then it fell into a well. A bucket of blue glass pulled it out of the well and put it on the right road. Finally, after a thousand vicissitudes, it arrived in a palace. Truth be told, the palace in question looked more like a tulip which had sprouted out of a decomposing skull than a well-arranged place. In fact, the staircase was laid out like a dead snake in the hall, and the upper stories were reached by means of an arrow which one stuck through one's rump and which the ground floor shot up to the desired level. There the letter found its addressee, who paced from one end of the stairway to the other without meeting "a living soul" and asked himself in which desert without caravans or camels, in which desert peopled only by the crackling noises of broken glasses, in which desert he had dragged his melancholy feet like an asparagus, a vegetable that, expecting to be eaten with French dressing, is only sucked with a white sauce. The unknown was no other than Clay Pipe, *famous for his duel with the empty bottles.*

It was then that I saw the light.

But perhaps it is worthwhile to tell of the marvelous adventures of *Clay Pipe* and the empty bottles.

Clay Pipe had always believed that virgins lived in shards of bottles. But having opened his left eye in one of them, he found he had been deceived and was quite vexed by it. Failing to find in the bottles the young virgins he was after, he resolved to raise the grandmothers suitably shriveled by a half century of usage. Is it necessary to say that his project miscarried miserably? Hardly had the grandmothers been shut up in the bottle shards when they turned into liquid and became in short order a sort of tar like that used to repair the streets of Paris. All hope thus to obtain a generation of small-sized grandmothers was lost.

But *Clay Pipe* was indefatigable. Without becoming discouraged, he sowed naval officers in the bottom of the bottles and that could have been his demise, for naval officers do not smoke clay pipes, but debris from ships and sailors' hair, which is bad for the health of empty bottles. *Clay Pipe* was not long in seeing the effect on his protégés, and he revenged himself on the naval officers, whom he reduced to the state of slugs, creatures much appreciated by empty bottles, as bottles eat a great many slugs, especially in the springtime. He was wrong, though, not to hide from the bottles the origin of their food; and the bottles, who in spite of everything were quite attached to the naval officers, became distinctly angry.

A duel with lanterns resulted and *Clay Pipe* was beaten, having swallowed only 721 lanterns while the smallest of his adversaries had devoured at least a thousand. Since that day *Clay Pipe* has paced the horizontal staircase from one end to the other in the hope of finding his empty bottles again, but in vain. They had fled long ago, thanks to the springtime sprouts of geraniums which grow so frequently in the stomachs of pregnant women, bringing on premature deliveries.

And the little white mole went away as she had come, like a crescent moon. I found myself alone again, desperately alone, my feet attached to a sort of sleigh which was decorated with a host of little pigs, who reminded me of the flag of the United States. This showed me that the sleigh was made of acorns and potato flour. While I reflected on the fragility of such a vehicle, it started to move while the pigs flew away, crying:

"Lafayette I am here!...Over there!...One doesn't make omelets without breaking eggs...eggs...eggs...eggs...eggs... eggs...eggs...Negroes have flat feet...Swedes eat mussels..." And a thousand other things in which the word "hair" was repeated often.

Only one young pig, glowing like a new coin, stayed on the sleigh, and when it stopped near the ear of a naturalized elephant, the pig addressed me as follows:

"I see into the toolhouses of road menders. I eat sleighs. I read Paul Bourget beginning at the end of each line. I play night-table music. I caress the fingers of brides and I keep a well-known politician in the forest of my silks. What is he, and who am I?"

But instead of replying to him, I asked:

"Did you have to stand in line?"

"Sit down, I beg of you," he replied, "I have had a little cold and now you're saved."

"I understand nothing of all this," I could not help telling him, here where cauliflowers litter the airless rooms and turn yellow when by chance the little crystal spiders happen to meet them, playing their customary game of whist in the evening in the deserted squares, despite the fact that the squares have been closed to the public for a long time. But this stupid beast would-n't let me go away so easily, and taking me aside asked:

"Does the gentleman want to put on his dressing gown?"

Hoping to get rid of him, I replied in the same silly tone he had adopted:

"I can't find my bedroom slippers."

Again the pig asked me:

"Does the gentleman wish me to comb his hair?"

"Just a part. I can do the rest of it very well," I replied, worn out.

Over the course of a few days, the sleigh slid rapidly between a double hedge of porcupines, who gravely contemplated our strange rig and fled as soon as we were out of sight, uttering cries so piercing that the frightened birds fell to the ground, where they remained flattened out like a piece of putty on a glass. I began to get worried, all the more so since an indefinable odor floated in the air, something like the smell of artichokes and like a well-groomed head of hair. And our speed, which increased steadily! And the pig, which had become as large as a church!

This animal upset me more than I could say, with his great pale face barred vertically with a sword, and a pistol tattooed on each side of an enormous nose, which supported a large cane, to which were attached more than fifty children's balloons. To tell the truth, these balloons, the purpose of which I did not understand, intrigued me considerably. For most contained within them a bearded man, whose chest was ornamented with myriad rusted decorations. His chest opened like a door, revealing an ash can teeming with enormous rats, which jostled and crushed one another, drawn no doubt by some alluring rottenness.

The pig, having observed my troubles and recommencing his questions, said to me:

"What is he, and who am I?"

"No doubt the inventor of a cattle car, so-called because it serves for the transportation of playing cards and principally clubs, like clovers, which must spread out in good season upon green fields, in order that they acquire the qualities of suppleness and endurance which other cards do not have."

The animal let out a great burst of laughter and murmured disdainfully:

"You're joking."

Then he commenced to sing:

> *On the prairie there is a lock*
> *a lock that I know*
> *It glows and rocks*
> *when the birds fly around*

On the prairie there is a camel
a camel with no teeth
I will make him some with a mirror
and his humps shall be my reward

On the prairie there is a pipe
where my destiny hides
On the prairie there is an armchair
And the tribunes will be at my feet
It will be warm, it will be cold

I will raise centipedes
which I will give to the dressmakers
and I will raise chair rungs
which I will give to bicycles

For a long time he continued in this manner, which was far from reassuring to me. Suddenly, as we approached a forest which had blocked the horizon for a long time, I saw the forest leave the ground and come galloping to our sides after having bowed with respect to my companion, who, at this moment, appeared to be filled with unbearable self-assurance. They had a long conversation from which I could grasp several words which gave me no idea of what it was about!

"…Down there, in this pavilion…what can these letters mean: S.G.D.G….If we should visit the naval section…provided that we should come safely into port…," etc.

However, I guessed that it had to do with me, and I had no doubt they intended to do me a bad turn, so I prepared to defend myself. I had no time for that. The forest grabbed me from behind, held me motionless for a second, then shoved my head into my stomach, glued my arms against my buttocks, and carried me away, rolling me like a barrel…

And since that day I have wandered over the world.

Translated by Elliot Paul

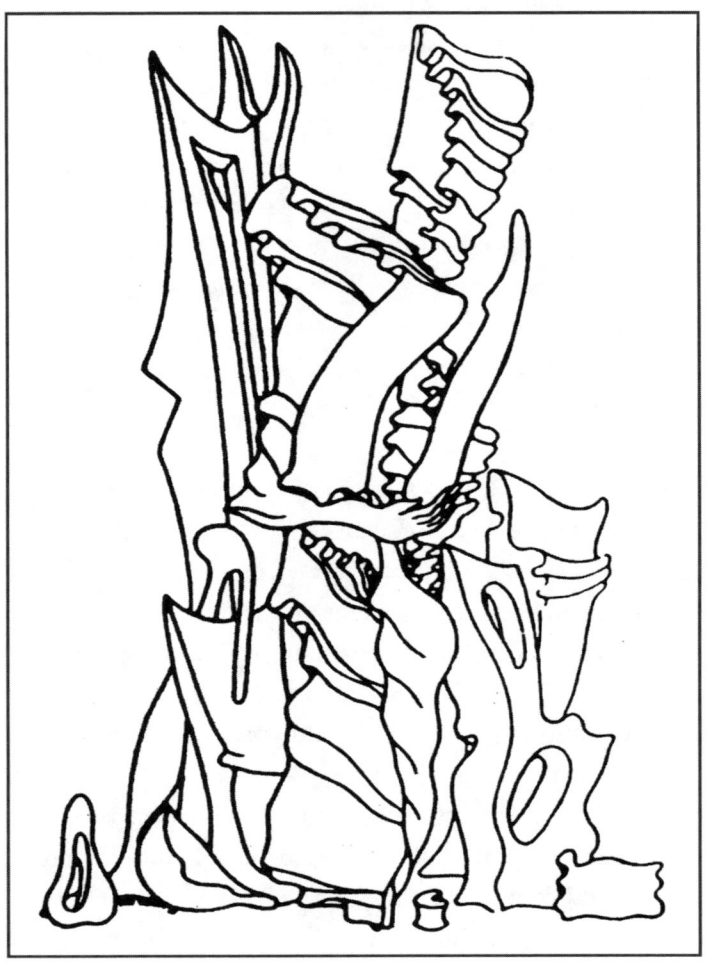

Yves Tanguy: Drawing for Péret's book
Three Cherries and a Sardine

BOSS OF THE CHAIR-RENTERS[1]

A S COCKROACHES PROFIT from the darkness to invade badly kept-up kitchens, today priests are cropping up all over in a world shadowed by a night growing more and more black. After the pastors of the music-hall, the working class ministers, the movie theater, radio, and television cassocks, now at Turin* the fashion designer priest has appeared. Certainly, the ecclesiastical sewers are overflowing at every corner in these sad years!

It is enough to recall that before the last war no priest could have lasted one day in a factory in the Paris region (he would have been immediately recognized for his true face as a cop and chased willy-nilly by the indignant workers) to measure the magnitude of the regression that this level of tolerance implies. As for trying to regulate fashion, no priest would have considered it, not even in fascist Italy! Fortunately, the delicious feminine vanity would have quickly done justice to the "models" blessed by this breed.

At the beginning of the century, the laws on the separation of church and state effectively contained the clerical wave to the domain of culture, morals, and customs. It is true that for the most enlightened of the ruling classes, the church then represented a blind rejection of the social progress that they pretended to promote. Since the last war, what a change! These same classes have lost all confidence in their future; they know that they survive only because they are not the object of an attack by the masses, and they profit from the reprieve thus granted to establish a zone of protection around them, entrusted to the most reactionary and obscurantist elements of society: the Church and the Army. The famous alliance of the cross and the sword is far from being dissolved, and the Indians of the Amazon continue to be right when they declare that the missionary heralds the soldier. If, as a consequence, they flee or, according to their mood, do away with the bad omen, who could hold a grudge against them and most of all, who doesn't envy them?

Translated by Madeleine Arenivar

Notes

1. In France, the chair-renter is a traditional employee of the church, usually a woman, who arranges the chairs in the church before mass and collects a fee from the parishioners based on the quality of their chair and where it is located.
L'Express, 22 January 1959. [Péret's note]

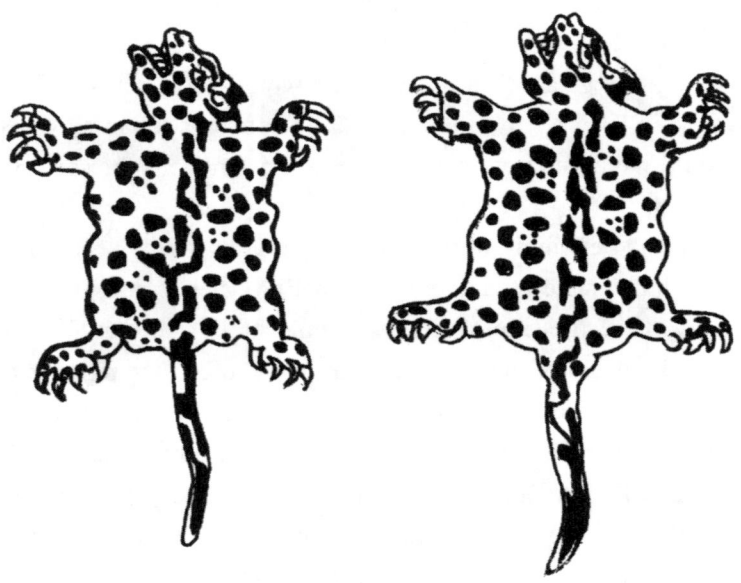

From the *Codex Mendoza*

NOTES ON PRE-COLUMBIAN ART

E QUIPPED EVERYWHERE with the same power, the eye, under the different latitudes of the world, contemplates a varied spectacle. If, for the man who rejects racial prejudices, the Negro is only distinguishable from the European, the Asian and the Indian by the degree of his intellectual development, it is no less true that the world in which he is born, lives and dies, determines the form of his culture and the rhythm of its development.

We have only to read Frazer to see that, in all times and places, the same myths haunt or have haunted humanity. The struggle of the eagle and the serpent, incorporated in the coat of arms of contemporary Mexico, can also be found in the Sumerian inscriptions made thousands of years before our period. The myth of the virgin mother which the Spanish conquerors brought to America along with all the evils of Europe flourished in the religious world of ancient Mexico under the name of Coatlicue and of Chimalma, immaculate mothers, one from Hiutzilopochtli, the other from Quetzalcoatl, and there is hardly any personality in Greco-Latin mythology which does not have its more or less exact counterpart in the Mexican or Mayan Olympus. From this it was only too easy to conclude that the American people had maintained relations at different periods with Europe, either through the agency of St. Thomas, identified by the Catholic priests with Quetzalcoatl, or because of the possible existence of Atlantis.

However, rejecting these overly-simple explanations, we are nonetheless impressed by the fact that, everywhere on the globe, man is passing or has passed through the same stages, and has endowed the same natural force with divinity before worshipping his subjugation of this force. The more primitive man has remained, the more his imagination has preserved its narrow ties with the immediately perceptible exterior world, in order subsequently to develop himself in a way that accords with the vividness of this perception. The exterior world acts on the imagination which, stimulated, reacts in turn on the exterior world and interprets it poetically before imperceptibly attempting to modify it according to its desires and needs. But this imagination wells up from an unconscious depth common to every man, and the primitive of today not only shows us what we were yesterday, but what we still really are underneath the cheap finery of modern education, and what the civilized man is vainly trying to forget: men still have hardly any more awareness of their own natures as they had in the remotest ages.

Art naturally follows the same path, for it is born of a desire to give form to the divinity that man has previously invented. Poetry, therefore, precedes plastic art, for man uses his imagination before possessing the means to give form to the creatures born of his desires and of his agonies. For this reason, it is a fact that in America, for example, the legends of the primitive peoples of the Amazon forest at the moment when they first discovered plastic art had a poetical richness which contrasts strangely with the poverty of the pre-Colombian Mexican myths known to us. Such Mexican myths contain a strong dose of philosophical commentary, making them relatively dry, whereas the art of pre-Columbian Mexico had developed to a level unsurpassed on any other part of the new continent.

It would not make sense to speak of art with reference to the pre-Colombian plastic production if we maintain the contemporary definition of this word—namely, that art is 'a disinterested activity of the mind' directed towards the creation of beauty. And by beauty here we mean exclusively the classical Greco-

66

Latin canon. Now it is obvious that the products of the pre-Colombian peoples do not answer to this definition, any more than does Negro sculpture, the works of any primitive people, the paintings of the Middle Ages, the sculpture of ancient Egypt, of China or of elsewhere. And yet no one, without showing a lack of understanding, blindness or prejudice, can avoid experiencing a real and profound emotion upon looking at some sculpture from Egypt, Oceania or from pre-Colombian America.

Does this emotion derive from the strangeness of the object or from its more or less slight connection with the classical art of western Europe? First we should observe that it is not generally the objects nearest to classical art which give the strongest affective shock, and that the sensation of strangeness grows as the object gets further from the classical model. It is also noticeable that the quality of this strangeness is not static or uniform, since one observer will be sensitive to one object rather than to another and since several observers placed in front of the same object will not all experience this sensation of strangeness, or they will feel it to varying degrees. It therefore follows that the strangeness of a given object is only relative. What is the reason for this relativity? This question can only be answered when we have been convinced of the superficial character of this sensation of strangeness. In fact it would appear that this apparent strangeness, as in the case of dreams, only serves to mask a deeper emotion. In other words, the feeling of strangeness is only the 'obvious content' of an emotion whose 'hidden content' is quite different, and linked to some repressed childhood memory which the sight of the object in question stimulates in the semi-darkness of the unconscious.

Certainly, the fairytales, the wonderful adventures which charmed our childhood years, teem with imaginary people, pre-mythical in a certain way, who are both man and beast and who comprise the child's private world. The adult taking stock of the exterior world, or more precisely, under the pressure of the exterior world into which he is integrating himself, gradually surrenders his childhood, the joys it gave him and the intuitive mode of knowledge which flowed out of it, replacing this intuitive mode of knowledge with rational knowledge alone. Furthermore, the adult man maintains an attitude of lofty condescension—condemnation even—towards his own childhood. This explains his feeling of surprise and alienation when he discovers that adults have known how to express similar conditions as those which he refuses to be reminded of. This is also the cause of the emotion that accompanies his surprise, showing itself all the more strongly the nearer and dearer his childhood is to him.

Pre-Colombian art is only strange in comparison with immediate reality, even though, in truth, this reality is not bereft of the marvelous. Therefore this art will fascinate artists and poets, whereas minds enamored of rationalism will only be sensitive to the achievements nearest to the classical ideal of western Europe. The poet and the artist always partake of the marvelous, the source of all beauty, in varying degrees. On the other hand, the rationalist mind rejects it, being in need of a continual contact with immediate exterior reality.

The unparalleled success of Greco-Latin art, which artistically satisfies a rationalist tendency, in full swing at the time of its creation, is surely due to this need for contact with the exterior world. But it is quite certain that amongst the Indians of pre-Colombian Mexico, the products of classical antiquity would have provoked a criticism very similar to that which Phidias would have made about some masterpiece of Aztec or Mayan art. Indeed, the pre-Colombian Indian speaks to the imagination in its own language, whereas the Greek sculptor first appeals to reason. Pre-Colombian art, therefore, corresponds more exactly to the deeper intentions of art than those Greco-Latin products which, by relegating imagination to a secondary place, overlook the principal source of all art.

The appetite for knowledge thus shows itself, in the first instance, as poetry; for man enjoys speech before he possesses the means of making an independent object of it. But this first poetry is entirely oriented towards explaining the exterior world, which man imagines to be made in his own likeness, obeying needs, impulses, desires and thoughts analogous to his own. The earth trembles with the anger of a raging giant whose fancy he can appease with appropriate offerings, just as the weakest tribe pays tribute to its more powerful neighbor, and as the rain is rebellious or docile to human complaints according to whether one knows or doesn't know the correct words with which to cajole it. For at first it is just a question of words transmitting a thought, the unquestioned effectivity of which preserves a strict communication between man and nature to which he knows he belongs. A mythical cultural cycle begins, which soon enriches itself with all the technical discoveries that a sedentary agricultural life will slowly make possible, albeit at the expense of its poetic inspiration. In the country with which we are concerned, the Indian first works wood with knives made of chips of obsidian, then clay which he models with a skill unparalleled throughout the world, and finally stone which he slowly learns to polish and to carve.

Art thus makes its first appearance as mythical poetry, and the images that man creates for himself at these moments represent both the supernatural beings of his own creation and the bond between him and these imaginary entities which will allow him to win them over. They are figures endowed with magic powers which a whole ritual of sorcery will set in motion. This is the starting-point of all religions. At the time of the Spanish conquest, the religions of the pre-Colombian Indians had not crystallized themselves around a singular belief; they were still permeated with a witchcraft and a magic found even now amongst the most developed modern religions.

***

According to a hypothesis still widely debated, despite the fact that it appears to be well founded, all of the Mexican and pre-Colombian Central American cultures have descended from a single mother-culture: the Olmecs, whose name was derived from *nahua ulmecatl* meaning: "men from the country of rubber." It hasn't yet been possible to fix a date, even approximately, for the Olmec invasion.

Salvador Toscano, a Mexican historian of pre-Colombian art, believes that an atmosphere of horror suffuses the art of the archaic period. This horror certainly does exist in some of the figures of the period but the predominating characteristics seem rather to be a grace, an elegance and a childish freshness that are only rarely found in the later periods, during which time this terrible and horrifying character does indeed develop, invading all pre-Colombian plastic art.

The co-existence of two such different tendencies in the oldest of the pre-Colombian Mexican cultures is easily explained, it seems to me, if one remembers that religious ideas are all born from the cult of the dead, which rests on an ambivalent feeling with regard to death. In fact, the physical terror inspired by death evokes the consoling idea that something of the dead man exists in an invisible world and that in various ways, from its position in this world, it assures the protection of those amongst the living who know how to win its favors. This ambivalent attitude, source of the idea of the soul, persists today among the Mexican people and expresses itself, for example, in

70

the exquisitely decorated sugar death's heads, marked with the name of the dead person, which are found in confectionery stores all over Mexico during All Saints' Day. However, this atmosphere of terror hardly existed in the archaic period, most likely because of the feeble development of religious ideas, which were probably limited at that time to their primordial magical expression, whereas later they constituted the very heart of pre-Colombian society.

The Indian of the archaic period was in direct contact with nature, which he had already explained in terms of poetry. Under the impulse of these primitive myths—myths almost completely emptied of moral sanction—Indians created, in a society in which the division of labor was still rudimentary, elegant terracotta statuettes that became much more sophisticated over time. There are probably hundreds of years that separate the coarse idols obtained by a process of *pastillage* from the delicately colored and modeled figures that are reproduced here.

Although we know almost nothing about the first people of the archaic period, we do know that the more recent peoples, immediately preceding or accompanying the first stages of the great Mexican civilizations, had already attained a relatively high level of culture. They were familiar with various materials and with the art of coloring them, and they had domestic animals, various gods, etc.

The final phases of archaic culture unfolded in conjunction with the beginning of the Teotihuacan civilization on the Central Mexican plateau, and with the birth of the Mayan civilization in the south, bordering Guatemala.

But another culture had already attained a higher level during the zenith of the archaic world: the Olmecs.

In distinction to the archaic figures and even to those of subsequent civilizations whose artistic products employ a symbolic language that we remain unable to decipher, Olmec statues sometimes show a startling naturalism, the expression of an inner life, which is hardly ever found before the appearance of the sensual and refined faces of the old Mayan Empire. Great violence and terrible brutality is often expressed and this contrasts in a striking way with the gently cheerful character of certain other sculptures. But if Olmec art seems to have attained its highest development in the archaic period, it is not archaic in its technique or in its quality. The Olmecs knew the art of carving and of polishing stone, as is proved by the enormous heads of La Venta or the magnificent figures in jade and in other rare stones that have been found all over Mexico. In contrast, the peoples of the archaic period only knew how to sculpt terra-cotta.

Olmec art marks a climax of horror and of terror and the victory of a religion with strict rites, served by an all-powerful caste of priests, over the primitive magic that defined previous periods; for horror and terror only obtain their civic rights in art with the advent of religion and the ever more complicated ritual fostered under the influence of priests. Even contemporary religions at the highest stage of their evolution still retain this imprint of their origins. Remember the goddess Kali or more recently Christ or The Sacred Heart!

It is curious to note that these Olmecs, whose influence on the art of the peoples of Teotihuacan is indisputable, have transmitted to them none of the brutal character particular to their art. The dominant note in the art of this civilization is a hieratic quality which brings it close to Egyptian art. The artists of Teotihuacan, like those of ancient Egypt, seem to have wished to give a generic, absolute and eternal image of the people of this period rather than an individual, circumstantial yet perishable image of man and of the godhead. This does not mean that there is no horror in it, but it denotes the impersonal expression of the Olmecs and it acquires an absolute and almost stereotyped character—a character that the later civilizations of the Central Mexican plateau were only partly able to rid their art of.

However, if religion necessarily stifles its own exuberance, imposing stricter limitations on the artist's imagination as its dogma becomes more elaborate, it produces in its period of ascendancy a new spirit: that of the grandiose and the sublime. In the pyramids of Egypt, the temples of classical antiquity or of India, the medieval cathedrals or the religious cities of Central Mexico, the Yucatan or of Guatemala, we discover this sense of the sublime which expresses itself in the magnificent proportions of Teotihuacan, Chichen Itza, Uxmal, Mitla, etc., where the use of vast open spaces so splendidly shows off the grandiose size of the temples. It is, perhaps, this sense of the sublime which most clearly distinguishes the great contemporary culture of Teotihuacan from its previous cultures, as we can see the openness to the sublime in the archaic pyramids of Cuicuilco and Copilco, as well as in the altars and giant heads of the Olmecs at La Venta, indicating the existence of a new material situation, bringing with it new psychological conditions for the peoples concerned.

In fact, we can be sure that the appearance of the grandiose in art marks the end of the creative period of mythical poetry and the appearance of rational ideas which first express themselves through the deification of heroes, for when mythical poetry has lost its power to create divinities, it acquires the power to celebrate heroes and to deify them. A new cultural cycle begins: the heroic cycle, which is having a renaissance today, with the celebration of false heroes, Hitler and Stalin, etc.

In other respects, the development of tribal life leads to a growing division of labor and to the formation of castes of warriors and of priests in opposition to the mass of producers, farmers and artisans. We can perhaps also find in this period the first signs of the slavery to which all the conquered were submitted. By awakening a feeling of power in the conqueror, the subjection of the conquered facilitates the birth of the cult of the hero, which rapidly attains its full development and which manifests itself in art in the tendency towards the sublime, noticeable in all the great Mexican civilizations as well as in Europe during the Middle Ages, when serfdom reached its zenith.

The warriors had to create divisions within various tribes so that one part of the tribe could serve as a defense corps to withstand the first assault, while the rest of the tribe could assemble to repel the invader; meanwhile, the priests, heirs to the old sorcerers, called on divine protection for the warriors and lay a curse on their enemies. This alliance of the priest and the warrior appears to be quite well established, indicating that it must have had a very remote origin and that it was firmly in place in the Teotihuacan civilization and amongst the Mayas of the old empire. This alliance still exists even in the most evolved modern civilizations, as is shown by the pejorative French expression condemning the *mariage du sabre et du goupillon*. It is true that at this time the alliance had a progressive character, since, protected by the arms of the warriors, the priests developed culture and the artisans developed their craft, whereas today it only serves to hinder all progress.

It is at this moment that fear and horror completely dominated the pre-Colombian religions, which surrounded themselves with a bloody ceremony, quite in harmony with the war-like customs of the tribes that founded these cults. Art naturally records an immediate reaction to this and the hieratic figures of Teotihuacan are almost completely superseded by savage figures which express the whole horror of these people, torn to pieces by continual wars, haunted by the unconscious fear of serving as an expiatory victim in some bloody sacrifice. The faces of the gods are convulsed, tortured and grimacing. Only the warriors' faces preserve a look of serenity in keeping with their caste, which exerted, in concert with the priests, an unlimited degree of power over the whole of society. The priestly caste was in control of the entirety of the intellectual and moral life of the people, the warriors included.

After the fall of Tollan, Central Mexico became a permanent battlefield until the arrival of the Spaniards. The Chichimecs were at perpetual war with all their neighbors, whom they dominated until the next rebellion of the Aztecs succeeded in breaking their yoke, dominating them in their turn and imposing Aztec power over the whole of the Mexican valley.

The most characteristic specimen of Aztec art is certainly the monument of Coalicue (she who has a skirt of snakes), the virgin mother of Huitzilopochtli, which immediately communicates an atmosphere of horror. With the Toltecs of Tollan and the Chichimecs, art only reflected insecurity, the agony of a life in which war was the daily feature; but with the Aztecs, war was the ultimate aim of life, which made it so that fear was the psychological axis of the whole people. In other words, if the life of the earlier peoples fostered an atmosphere of terror which reflected itself in their art; the Aztecs made a virtue of horror, and turned it into an instrument of material and moral domination. Their sculpture was clearly aimed at inspiring this terror, which in reality was only a product of their own unconscious horror. In other words, the exteriorization of this horror in art is only an attempt to dominate it.

At this time, the pre-Colombian world underwent fundamental modifications. After the collapse of Teotihuacan, slavery and servitude attained considerable proportions and all the tribes of the district were subjected to it in turn. Furthermore, those tribes, whose independence could only be preserved by struggle, maintained a war-like tradition which is expressed by their god Huitzilopochtli, derived from a solar myth. This god is, in fact, the image of the sun, a warrior permanently triumphing over darkness. Now it is the custom of primitives to try to scare the adversary in order to assure themselves more easily of victory. There is nothing astonishing in the fact that these aggressive habits, as yet unrelieved by a long sedentary existence, should have had their effects on the entirety of the collective life of the people, including in their religion and art. Amongst the people descended from Teotihuacan, war was, in reality, the focal point of the preoccupations of the tribe, and also the highest standard of value. Even religion was subservient to it; if peace was pro- longed, it was necessary to arrange sham fights between neigh- boring tribes in order, in the course of imaginary battles, to take prisoners as sacrifices for the gods. Moreover, amongst the Aztecs, women who died in childbirth had access to the holy place of Huitzilopochtli, for they were considered to be warriors fallen on the field of battle.

However, alongside the peoples of the valley of Mexico, heirs and bearers of an advanced culture, lived peoples whose art had undergone a much slower evolution. The Tarascans, despite having learned the art of working stone and metal thanks to the Toltecs, had chiefly continued to model the earth. The techniques of the other peoples and their more finished art had only a small hold over them. Sometimes their figures, worked according to the old method of *pastillage*, show an artistic skill in great con- trast to the poverty of the means employed; sometimes, on the contrary, their figures show a very advanced technique, as well as a survival of the most archaic types. This irregular progress is probably due to the Tarascans' remoteness from the great centers of civilization—an isolation which, in their case, favored a kind of hermetic evolution. The existence of polygamy, still practiced by them at the arrival of the Spaniards, in distinction to the monogamy of the 'nahuas' of the valley of Mexico, clearly shows the slowness of their evolution. In comparison with the archaic peoples of this region whose art already showed a grace and an elegance attesting a regular and harmonious development, fruit of a relatively happy and easy existence, the Tarascan figures have a monstrous appearance. They have a close similarity to the pictures drawn by children, and express primitive terrors which no poetical explanation can elucidate. The most striking example of this infantilism is given by the illustration of a woman in childbirth, whose baby is being born from the navel.

***

In its initial periods, pre-Colombian art is defined by a search for ever more appealing stereotypes—a search that, at least amongst the cultures of the central plateau, continues up through the end of the archaic period. This tendency probably resulted from the need that society felt to identify idealized mythical beings. The identification of such beings was almost certainly accompanied by increasingly severe and complex religious rites, which were themselves linked to the birth of a priestly caste.

The attributes with which these images are adorned evolve in a similar manner until the moment when man, far from his original image—the image having reached the end of its evolution—discovers the symbol, makes himself abstract, and develops a handwriting that permits the more-or-less exact transcription of already-acquired knowledge, and its use with a view to further progress. A process of changing over from intuitive knowledge to rational knowledge takes place, which relegates art to a secondary role. A parallel procedure takes place on the pure-

ly artistic level, consisting of an attempt to detach art from its re-
ligious basis. From the end of the archaic period onwards, we
can see an attempt at the realistic representation of the human
model.

The Olmecs, having a more advanced culture, had arrived
at this point early on. There is evidence that the Olmecs kept
their more archaic art alive in the way that we keep "traditional"
arts alive. This is one way to explain the persistence of the image
of the man with the jaguar face in Olmec art. Olmec culture, or,
at any rate, some of its elements, fertilized the last phase of ar-
chaic culture from which Teotihuacan was born, and, at the same
time, it continued amongst the Mayans of the old empire, whose
hieroglyphs were very similar to those of the Olmecs.

After this moment of cross-fertilization, we notice a rela-
tive stagnation of art. Even if the civilizations succeeding the
Olmec culture contributed their own particular genius, they al-
most entirely limited themselves to refining the former discover-
ies up to the time when decadence appeared and when new,
younger and more energetic people took possession of the former
culture. The appearance at each stage of stereotyped figures,
more or less derived from former creations but incorporating
new features, shows both the slow pace of cultural development
and the persistence of an effort which was completely destroyed
by the Spanish invasion. But would the pre-Colombian cultures
have been able to progress to the level of Europe, deprived as
they were of material means? In any case the rhythm of their
evolution would have remained very slow, but this was no reason
to destroy them.

Translated by Peter Watson

THE SUNDAY REBEL

A Critique of Camus

SOCIAL MAN IS born of rebellion. It is through rebellion that man asserts his true being, the essential quality which sets him above the rest of nature, the ability to control his own destiny (since in rejecting a previous state of affairs he reveals his will to choose), and that he offers the only guarantee he can give—his life—so that social life can exist. This rebellion, as Camus says, implies a no and a yes. No to injustice and oppression—a resounding "no" that drowns out the still hesitant "yes" of justice and freedom.

However, this moment of rebellion did not come about all at once, like a dew-laden mushroom in the dawn of man's social being; man had to wander a long way through the underground labyrinth of his own nature, beset right and left by the obstacles of superstition, stumbling over routine, sliding into the abysses of religions. This is because he had no previously formed social thinking to rely on, since he was not yet the social man whom rebellion awakens. Instead, he had only his own human intuition as he sought his identity in the dark recesses of his mind, whose shadows rebellion would, when it arrived, begin to drive away. In this labyrinth, which would ultimately lead him from the herd to a fledgling social awareness, man in his despair could only feel a deep resentment of the forces crushing him. What use would this feeling be to him? At this stage, he does not know, but instinctively, just in case, he clings to it. He is right, because being still entirely governed by his emotions, this is all he has.

In fact, if rebellion is born of an intolerable situation which must be done away with, it nevertheless has its roots in a complex of emotions whose driving force is resentment. However, it is only insofar as this complex of emotions is overcome that rebellion can be born, for resentment, directly expressed, can only lead to vengeance.

Rebellion bursts out at the moment when this complex of emotions is dominated, when vengeance is sublimated; in short, it marks man's transition from an individual emotional level to the collective level, where he stands out as a social being, even if his rebellion can only be expressed in an individual action, since this action translates, or aims to translate, a collective desire consisting above all in the rejection of a situation which has engendered rebellion.

This refusal, in turn, is made up of various factors: condemnation of the injustice done to the man, desire for a situation from which this injustice has been banned, desire for freedom. The slave wants to abolish slavery, the proletarian wants to abolish the proletariat; both systems are an attack on justice and freedom, but beneath the rebellion of the slave or the proletarian lies a new desire which has not yet found a means of expressing itself, even though it is the very soul of rebellion: equality. "You are only a man, like me, no more than me," says the slave to the master, the worker to the capitalist (as the helot of the Stalinist counter-revolution will one day say to the agent of the N.K.-V.D.), "I am your equal."

Rebellion implies then a threefold aspiration: For justice, freedom and equality; but of the three demands only one, equality, guarantees the practicability of the other two, although in rebellion equality is implicit rather than openly formulated. In fact this rebellion develops at first in a vague atmosphere, a world with undefined limits where affect reaches out towards conscience. We might say it is a compromise between passion rejecting injustice and conscience aspiring towards equality. That is why rebellion seeks above all to abolish the situation it rose against, without planning at the outset to replace it. Therefore it cannot lead to the overthrow of the situation which engendered it, only, at best, to its attenuation. And moreover, this attenuation can be achieved temporarily only if the rebellion is powerful enough to impose it and to force the oppressor to make concessions which he will abide by, as long as he fears rebellion.

When Dreux-Brésé said to Louis XVI, "It is not a rebellion, it is a revolution," he summed up in one phrase the whole distance which separates the two. Rebellion in fact explicitly desires only that the state which led to it will cease, but does not know what it should be replaced by, or even if a different state of affairs can be substituted for the one which caused it. Revolution, on the other hand, gives this rebellion an aim without which it can achieve nothing. To the negative formulations of rebellion, revolution adds positive statements: down with oppression, down with injustice, freedom through equality. So revolution is a higher form of rebellion, a rebellion which has kept its medium of passion while giving itself a conscious aim; the revolutionary is a rebel who has matured, since he knows not only what he wishes to abolish, but also what he is seeking to realize. So Camus is right in saying: "The revolutionary is also a rebel or he is not a revolutionary." One should even say that there is no revolutionary who is not a rebel and the revolutionary who claims he is not motivated by rebellion is merely a potential bureaucrat, in actual fact a counter-revolutionary.

Camus' work aims to analyze rebellion in each of its forms, expressions and results. This goal is ambitious in the extreme and presupposes, as far as society is concerned, a detailed examination of all the forms of rebellion and the revolutionary ideas they gave rise to. Did Camus actually undertake this study? Fontenis argued in *Le Libertaire* on January 4th 1952 that Camus' knowledge of anarchy in general and Bakunin in particular is extremely rudimentary—probably, we might add, limited to a reading of the *Hisory of Anarchy*. Nora Mitrani has shown in *La revolt en question*, that he knew little of Sade except some quotations taken here and there (from Klossowski?), including from her own writings. Camus, in reproducing a part of Mitrani's text that contained an unfortunate printer's error—a matter of misplaced quotation marks—scrupulously maintained the error in *The Rebel*. Hard lines. It is obvious too that he has studied Marx no more closely than Bakunin or Sade; that's perfectly clear. At the very most he is acquainted with Marx through Stalinist publications which use him, G.P.U. style, and through the quotations of his commentators and critics. In his references to Marx, and particularly his chapter on "state terrorism and rational terror," it seems that Camus drew heavily on Jules Monnerot's *Sociology of Communism*.[1]

It is easy to notice the similarities between the two texts and the ideas they express. However the important difference between the two lies in the fact that Monnerot criticizes Marx after studying him, whereas Camus has no knowledge of Marx, but takes from Monnerot what he needs for his polemic against Marx. In passing, we must reply to Monnerot—and through him to Camus, that human history has been and still is to a great extent the history of man's class struggles on the social level. It has been so since the advent of class-based societies and will remain so until the establishment of a classless society.

From that time on, history will deal with what lies outside the history of class struggles and probably also with other things beyond our imagination, but it is obvious that the classless society does not mark the end of history. At the very most this epoch marks the end of history dominated by the history of class struggles, just as our contemporary history marked the end of history as legend, in which signs of the history of class struggles could sometimes already be detected.

Only compare, on the one hand, the standard of living, freedom and culture reached at the beginning of this century in capitalist society to the high point of any other society, and, on the other hand, the present condition of the helots of Stalinism to that of slaves in the worst periods of history, in the most barbarous societies that ever existed. In which environment did we see a boy of seventeen sentenced to five years' hard labor camp for having, while in Poland, illegally crossed the border of the "workers' homeland" to escape from Hitler's invasion armies? And all this only to die thirteen years later in those same camps, after an additional sentence of ten more years' internment? And the degeneration of capitalism, of which Russia is an integral part, is only beginning.

The same applies to Marx's ideas as to all ideas which are inevitably the product of the age in which they were expressed. They contain a transient element, since they were limited by the knowledge of their times. Part of Monnerot's work represents an attempt to criticize Marx and Marxism and we can only regret that this was not coupled with positive proposals. We cannot say the same of Camus since *The Rebel*, in spite of its pretentious wrapper, does not aim to "understand our times" but to adapt our times to the ideas of Camus. Exactly what he accuses several Marxists of doing! Just as they see Marx through the eyes of the faithful, so Camus makes anti-Marxism an article of faith. The one is no better than the other. However, one should not reject Marx on the grounds that some of his ideas are out of date or reflect a way of thinking which his heirs have not adequately brought up to date as they gained more and more knowledge. Marx is fundamental to the revolutionary and socialist thinking of the last century. He has to be subjected to the same kind of criticism as he imposed on his own predecessors and contemporaries, so that the vital elements of each (and I am thinking in particular of libertarian ideas) might find their place in a theory better suited to the demands of our times.

Throughout his work, Marx insisted on the necessity for social revolution as the means of attaining a new, superior form of society, which would entail the abolition of all injustice and oppression. At first sight there seems to be a contradiction between the end aimed at—a society without violence—and the violence of revolution. But how else can the "infernal cycle" Camus speaks of be broken? In fact, the violence of revolution is merely the response to the permanent violence of capitalist society. It is the action of the condemned man strangling his warder to get back his freedom.

Marx's insistence on this point is enough for Camus to call it a prophecy and go on to speak of its failure, even though he declares later on that "after the revolution of 1917," a soviet Germany "would have opened heaven's door." Thus, we should not speak of social revolution as a prophecy, but rather as a prospect, and an immediate one at that. We know that the failure of the German revolution, probably engineered by nascent Stalinism, whose reactionary interests were opposed to this revolution, marked the beginning of the revolutionary ebb-tide. The workers returned to the attack in 1936, beginning in Spain, but they found their opponent, not in the bourgeoisie, which with the exception of Franco was resigned to its fate, but in Stalinism.[2] It is significant that Camus does not once mention the Spanish revolution. If he does not mention it, is it not because he has failed to make it fit with his argument, as the Spanish revolution by itself is enough to destroy his poisonous cocktail of Marxism and Stalinism? Or is it because, as a member of the "antifascist" resistance, which went along with Stalinism under duress, all he saw of the Spanish revolution was the Stalinist opposition to Franco?

No one will deny that the failure of the revolution in Germany and in western Europe, at the end of the 1914-1918 war, followed by the Stalinist counter-revolution and finally the failure of the Spanish revolution, posed problems which Marx, not being Nostradamus, could not foresee. "First of all, the economic evolution of the contemporary world proves many of Marx's postulates to be unfounded," says Camus. Marx could only make hypotheses for the immediate future; he never once declared that these hypotheses would be valid forever. Logically, social revolution would bring the period he was examining to a close. This not having yet occurred, it remains on the agenda, but in the context of a new period of capitalism, that of the degeneration of the system.

If, in Marx's day, it was possible to foresee an indefinite concentration of capital, Camus has only to open his eyes to see that this is in fact the condition that we find ourselves in today. It has even been perfected in Russia, since everything belongs to the State; even the people, who are answerable directly to the police. This concentration of the capital in the hands of the State is a sign of social degeneration, which was itself inevitable because of the failure of the revolution and which is destined to continue indefinitely if revolution does not halt this trend. The same is true of the nationalism that Camus invokes against Marx. Its present aggravated form is merely a consequence of advancing social decay.

History is now engaged in a sprint between social degeneration and revolution, and in this race, burdened as it is with Stalinism and the weight of corpses from the October and Spanish revolutions, revolution is off to a bad start. On the other hand, history has granted revolutionaries a little more time. But once this time is up, the only outlook for society will be the slow rotting of civilizations, as they find themselves unable to locate the reserves of strength needed to go beyond themselves and be renewed in a higher form.

Rebellion and revolution are closely linked today. In fact, any separation of the two is always more or less arbitrary, for the workers have a sense—when they do not actually know—of what needs to be done. In June 1936, who launched the movement to occupy the factories? No-one. In this event, leaders Blum, and Thores too, while paying lip-service to the movement, sabotaged it by establishing the "moderation" advocated by Camus, thus preventing rebellion from changing into revolution. Is this what Camus is aiming at? It seems not. He simply wants to play, to juggle with rebellion, anarchy and Marxism; but he is playing with fire. And in this game Camus has burned himself, and only the ashes remain.

(excerpts)

Translated by Sandra Wright and Alice Mayoux

Notes

1. Among other points, the imperialist ambitions of Stalinism, the Messianic quality attributed to Marx, the opposition between the latter and the Greek way of thinking, the relations between Marxism and Christianity, the role of revolutionary trade-unionism.
2. See Grandizo Munis: *Jalones de derota: promesa de victoria.* Mexico: Editorial "Lucha Obrera," 1947.

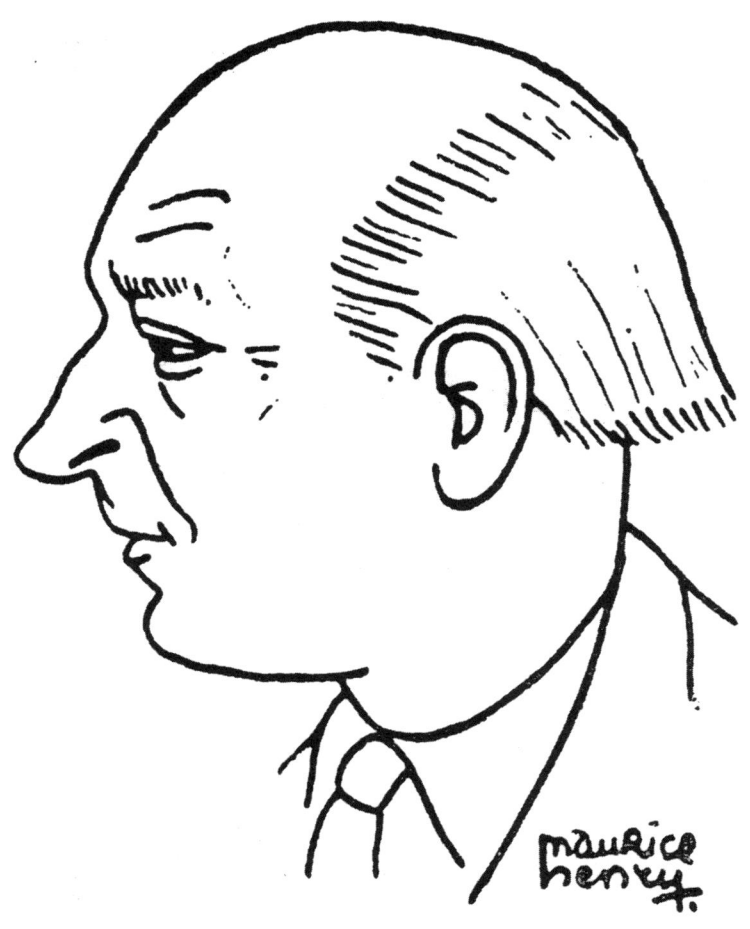

Maurice Henry: Péret

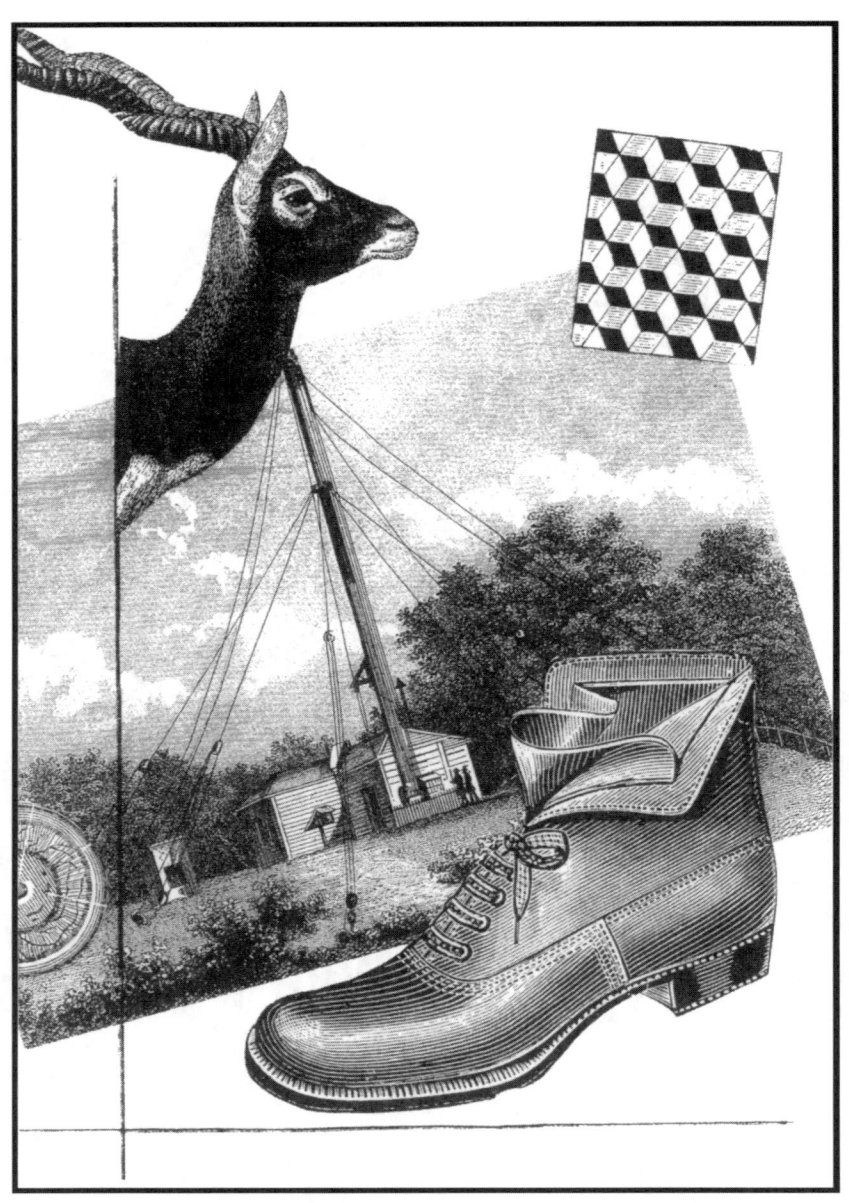

Joel Williams: Tribute to Péret

MAGIC: THE FLESH AND BLOOD OF POETRY

I

BIRDS FLY, fishes swim, and man invents. He alone possesses the imagination and thus is always alert, always stimulated by a necessity constantly being renewed. He knows that his sleep swarms with dreams which advise him to kill his enemy the very next day, or that, interpreted according to the rules, outline his future. But are they his dreams, the manifestations of his "spirit?" Or do they emanate from some ancestor who is favorably disposed towards him or seeks vengeance for some offense? According to the conception of primitive man, dreams are not really dreams—this mysterious activity of the mind in an inert body reveals to him that his "double" is watching over him, or that an ancestor is influencing his destiny or, later, that a god—Viracocha of the Incas, Huitsilopoctli of the Aztecs—desires the happiness of the people in exchange for an offering of adoration.

Primitive man, knowing the narrow limits of his physical possibilities, is not so presumptuous as to believe that the spirit animating him night and day belongs to him alone. The sun, moon, stars indeed, all Nature, are kindred to him, and if, from a material standpoint, he is weak, he is compensated spiritually by a power he believes to be infinite. It is enough for him to find the adequate means of reaching the spirit, which he must ultimately master. If Nature seems hostile or at least indifferent to the fate of man, it has not always seemed so. Animals, plants, meteorological phenomena and the stars were all seen as ancestors ready to rescue or punish him. They were, in this early stage, seen as good or bad, and were only later transformed from symbols of reward or condemnation into things that were seen as being either useful or harmful to man. This "demythologization" was thoroughgoing—only a few natural phenomena are now explained through mythical narratives. Faced with a hailstorm, the Breton peasant still says, "The Devil is beating his wife!"—a phrase which indicates that this conception of the world is not unfamiliar to him and that he can still see Nature with the eyes of a poet. *Still*, the barbarous society of our time, which forces men to "live" on canned food and—so to speak—cans them in rooms the size of a coffin, putting a premium on sun and sea, tries to reduce their intellectual level to that existing in the immemorial time prior to the recognition of poetry. I am referring to the wretched existence that present-day society imposes on workmen—an existence portrayed by Charlie Chaplin in "Modern Times." For these men, poetry irrevocably loses its meaning. All they have left is language. Their masters have not taken this away because language is still necessary. But they have emasculated it so that it no longer has any poetic expressiveness and has sunk to the degenerate level of talk between debtor and creditor.

While it is indisputable that language, produced automatically as a result of the need for mutual communication between men, first tends to satisfy this need for human relationship, it is no less true that men begin to use entirely poetical forms to express themselves as soon as they have—in a purely unconscious manner—succeeded in organizing their language, in adapting it to their most urgent necessities, and have realized the possibilities it conceals. In a word, as soon as the primordial need for communication is satisfied, language becomes poetry.

So-called primitive men—even the most backward tribes—have by now lost sight of the distant epoch when language was invented. Here and there, some legendary fragment poetically recalls this discovery, but very faintly. However, the richness and variety of cosmic interpretations which primitive men have invented prove the vigor and freshness of the imagination of such peoples. These interpretations show that savages do not doubt that "language was given to man to use surrealistically" (André Breton: *Manifesto of Surrealism*) and to complete the satisfaction of their desires. Indeed, the man of prehistoric times could think only in poetic terms and, in spite of his ignorance, penetrated, perhaps intuitively, into himself and into Nature (with which he has such deep kinship), going much further than the rationalistic thinker who analyzes Nature with his bookish knowledge.

There is no need here to write a defense of poetry at the expense of rational thinking. But I do protest against the scorn in which poetry is held by the champions of logic and reason. Both logic and reason were discoveries that had their origin in the subconscious mind. The invention of wine did not lead men to bathe in wine instead of water, and no one will contradict the fact that without rain, wine could never have existed. Likewise, without the illumination of the subconscious, logic and reason, still in limbo, could not be used to disparage a poetry that had not yet been created. As long as we do not unreservedly recognize the capital role of the subconscious in our physical life, its effects on the conscious mind and the reactions of the latter on the former, we shall continue to think like a priest, that is, like a dualistic savage, with, however, the following reservation—that the savage remains a poet, while the nationalist, who refuses to understand the *unity* of thought, impedes cultural movement. On the other hand, if he does understand it, the rationalist becomes a revolutionist who, perhaps without knowing it, tries to come back to poetry. We must, once and for all, break down the artificial opposition created by sectarian minds on either side of the barricade that they have collaboratively erected—a barricade between poetic thought (qualified as pre-logical) and logical thought, between rational and irrational thought.

A century before Freud, Goethe confirmed the popular belief that poets are the precursors of learned men and said that "man can no longer remain in a conscious state of mind but must plunge again into the subconscious because that is where the root of his being lives."

Prehistoric man's conscious thought, emerging from the fog of the subconscious, is scarcely different from animal instinct. The conscious thought of the primitive man of today is still very weak. It is strictly limited to the practical necessities of everyday life. Subconscious and oneiromantic activity dominates it completely. But can we say that civilized man—in spite of what is said or supposed—is so far away from his "inferior" brother? Certainly, the explanations which primitive man gives of the world, himself, and Nature are products of pure imagination in which the part of conscious thought is nil or almost so. That is doubtless why his creations, unrestricted, uncritiqued, touch the poetic marvelous.

II

No doubt I should define what I mean by "the poetic marvelous." But I shall do nothing of the sort! It has a luminous quality which cannot stand the competition of the sun; it dispels shadows and the sun dulls its brightness. The dictionary, of course, limits the definition of this word to its dry etymology—and gives no more idea of "marvelous" than an orchid, pressed in a book, gives the impression of its living splendor. I shall try only to suggest what the "poetic marvelous" means.

Sometimes the dolls of the Hopi Indians of New Mexico have heads which represent, schematically, a medieval castle. I shall try to enter this castle. There are no doors; the ramparts have the thickness of a thousand centuries. It is not in ruins, as you might think. Since the time of Romanticism, the ramparts have risen again, reconstituted like rubies, and as hard as that gem. Now that I butt my head against the ramparts I find they have the ruby's limpidity too. They open like high grasses giving way to the passage of a wild beast. Then, by some effect of osmosis, I find myself inside, emitting rays like the Aurora Borealis. Glittering statues of armor, standing guard in the hall like a row of mountain peaks eternally covered with snow, salute me with raised fists whose fingers shed a continual flux of bird feathers, made up of the delicate plumage of hummingbirds and birds of paradise (unless they are falling stars, coupled so as to obtain this mixture of primary colors). Although I seem to be quite alone, I am surrounded by a crowd which blindly obeys me. These are beings less distinct than motes in a sunbeam. In their heads made of roots, their firefly eyes dart in every direction and, with their twelve wings armed with claws, they move as fast as the lightning which trails in their wake. They stand in my hand, eating the eyes of peacock feathers. If I press them between my thumb and index finger I end up with a rolled cigarette, which, between the feet of a knight in armor, quickly takes the form of an artichoke.

The poetic marvelous is everywhere, hidden from vulgar eyes, but ready to burst like a time-bomb. I open a drawer and see, between spools of thread and a pair of compasses, a spoon for absinthe. Through the holes of this spoon I see a band of tulips, marching in goosestep fashion. Philosophy professors stand in their corollas, discussing the categorical imperative. Each of their words, demonetized coins, break in pieces on the ground, which bristles with noses—and the noses throw the words back in the air where they turn into smoke rings. Their slow dissolution engenders minute fragments of mirrors which reflect a bit of wet moss.

But what was I saying… Why open a drawer if a scorpion, falling from the ceiling to my table, says to me: "Don't you know me? I'm the old lamplighter. I left my wooden leg in a vacant lot where an old burnt-down factory is crumbling in ruins, while its high chimney, which still stands, knits brightly colored sweaters. Since then my wooden leg has made its way. Look at the alderman's bay-window, this 'Bide-a-Wee' on its head, these… But you easily recognize a pope who quickly hides a monocle in his left hand. The monocle can only be a poisoned host. Meanwhile, with his right hand, he traces the sign of the cross in the air—but backwards. At this gesture, the chimney splits open from top to bottom like a mussel, revealing its sixteen floors, where naked ballerinas, somewhat more dense than a whirlwind of pollen, repeat lascivious and complicated steps in the eye of a cat." And the scorpion, having stung itself with its tail, dug down into the thickness of my table, ornamenting it with an inkspot in which I could read with the aid of a mirror: "Hair hangman."

The poetic marvelous is everywhere, in every period of history, in every instant of time. It is, or rather it should be, life itself—it being understood that this life should not deliberately be made sordid, as our present society makes it with its schools, religion, courts, wars, occupations and liberations, concentration camps, and horrible material and intellectual poverty. However, I remember: it was the prison of Rennes where *they* locked me up in May, 1940. I had committed the crime of thinking that this society was my enemy because for the second time in my life—like so many others—I was obliged to defend it, although I did not recognize anything in common with it.

You know how a prison cell is furnished: there is a bad imitation of a bed which during daytime must be folded up against the wall—so that if you want to rest, you must stretch out on the

94

floor—and a table fixed to the wall opposite the bed, and near it, a stool fixed to the same wall so that the prisoner will not yield to the temptation of flinging it at his jailer.

One morning the window of my cell was painted blue. The window was high up, out of my reach. I spent most of the day stretched out on the floor, my head turned towards the window where the sunlight could no longer penetrate. Sometime after the panes had been painted I saw a picture of Francis the First on one of them—a picture I might have remembered from my elementary history book. On the next pane was a horse that reared. Then there was a tropical landscape such as Rousseau might have painted and in the lower right hand pane appeared a sprite —a charming sprite, who tossed butterflies over her head with a light, graceful gesture. In the last pane I read the number 22 and immediately knew I should be freed on the 22nd. But the 22nd of what month, what year? It was then the first week of June, 1940. The crime I was accused of was then severely punished and my most optimistic prospect was three years in prison. Nevertheless, I was forthwith convinced, despite the probability to the contrary, that my liberation was near.

However, every day—or almost every day—the pictures changed. I never saw more than four panes at once on the eight panes. Francis the First turned into a boat sinking beneath the waves; the landscape, a complicated machine; the horse, a room in a café, etc. But the figure 22 remained obstinately visible until a bomb fell one day from a plane, shattering the morale of the jailers—who disappeared for the whole day—and most of the panes. The only one that was left—and that only in part—was the pane on which I continued to see the number 22. Once or twice it disappeared to show up elsewhere.

Believe it or not, I got out of the Rennes prison on July 22nd—by paying a ransom of a thousand francs to the Nazis.

Free—and enchanted with my "discovery," I painted panes in blue, green, red, etc.,—but all I saw, alas, was solid color.

The error was flagrant; marvels cannot be made according to a druggist's formula. They always take you by surprise. A certain state of "vacancy" is necessary too, before they can happen. Of course, I hear you saying: "See—that's just what I thought. It was only an illusion on your part." But the fellow who splashed the panes with big brush strokes never could have painted the pictures I saw later. Yet they were so real I could not doubt for a moment but that I had seen them. And how is it that when I colored the panes, no pictures appeared?

In prison, I was in that state of vacancy I have just referred to, I was "one of those whose desires have the form of clouds" (Charles Baudelaire).

All the pictures I saw on the first day (they are the only ones I shall take into account as I do not remember the others so clearly; I got into the habit of looking for them each day, whereas the first ones took me by surprise), were based on my sharp appetite for liberty. That was quite natural for a person in my situation. The picture of Francis the First immediately suggested the school where I had first learned about this king; the history books presented him as a kindly liberal sovereign, the protector of artists and poets of the Renaissance. The idea of that school came to mind because it too had been a prison—one from which I was released each evening and which, in retrospect, was so much more preferable than that of Rennes! The teacher too was a sort of jailer—but how much more good-natured than the men I had to deal with day and night!

The rearing horse symbolized my ineffectual protest against my unfortunate predicament. It was also reminiscent of the fact that in the previous war I had met the enemy while serving in the first regiment cuirassiers. What penal servitude that regiment was, too! The officials had only the most vulgar insults and threats of punishment for their men. Still, the soldiers had a few hours of liberty each day which made their lot—execrable as it was—preferable to that of a prisoner.

Now as to the Rousseau-like tropical forest, with sprite and butterflies—Rousseau had belonged to the French expeditionary force sent to Mexico by Napoleon III. The memory of his stay there had inspired his tropical backgrounds. Before the present war, which I knew was coming, and which I knew would be dangerous for me because of the military dictatorship in France that it would bring about, I tried in vain to go to Mexico. For a long time I had wanted to know this country—which now has given me a refuge.

The sprite immediately brought to mind the thought of my companion. I had not had any news about her, and her fate worried me much more than my own. I knew she was menaced both by internment in a French camp and expulsion—which would have meant a concentration camp. I could not forget the expression of terrified distress which I had seen on her face when I had left her, eight or ten days before in Paris. She was standing on the platform of the Gare Montaparnasse when I, handcuffed and surrounded by an imposing escort of policemen, had boarded the train for Rennes. All these sad thoughts—which I might liken to black butterflies—were being cast away by the sprite. True, the butterflies on the pane were light colored—but my companion had always suffered from a nervous fear of insects, even of butterflies. I had often joked with her about this, saying: "In tropical countries there are often actual clouds of butterflies. What would become of you if we were ever to go to Mexico?" My companion's presence in the exotic landscape proved how much I wanted her to be free, out of reach of the dastardly police. Certainly, it would be better for her to ward off light-colored butterflies than the "black butterflies" which must be attacking her day and night. Finally, if we had succeeded in leaving for Mexico, we would be free, and what would even a cloud of butterflies matter!

III

The poet's status is such that he who lays claim to it is automatically placed on the fringe of society, and this is the case the more truly he is a poet. The recognition of "accursed" poets clearly shows this. They are "accursed" for being outside the pale of society—just as their predecessors, the sorcerers, were outlawed by society and its church for the same reasons. The sorcerers undermined the religion-dominated medieval society with their intuitions, and today poets combat with their visions the intellectual and moral postulates which present-day society would surreptitiously like to give a religious character. Orderly people consider poets to be madmen because of their visionary nature. In primitive societies, madmen were thought to be ambassadors from heaven or messengers from the infernal powers. But their supernatural power was never doubted. Thus, we can say that the sorcerer, the poet and the madman have a common denominator. But the madman, having broken off with the exterior world, drifts on the wild ocean of his imagination and we cannot see what he is looking at.

The common denominator of the sorcerer, the poet and the madman cannot be anything else but magic...the flesh and blood of poetry. Moreover, at the time that magic summed up all of human science, poetry was not distinguished from it; thus we can say, without any risk of error, that primitive myths are largely made up of the residue of poetic illuminations, intuitions or omens confirmed in such a brilliant manner that they instantaneously penetrated to the depths of these peoples' consciousness.

The origin of poetry is lost in the unfathomable depths of ages because man was born a poet—a fact that children prove every day. But poetry was the great revolution—the first historic, or rather, prehistoric revolution—in which the incest taboo played the leading role. It was this taboo which gave the revolution its initial impetus by directing a part of the libido towards an outlet from which it emerged, sublimated, in the form of the myth, projecting the picture of the assassinated father on the infinity of the heavens. "The corpse of a dead enemy always smells good." Though disgraced in his lifetime, the father is honored by his murderers with a legendary halo which succeeding generations will enhance with new light. Such are the first myths, the first poems of those distant times when all men were more or less sorcerers—that is, poets and artists.

Naturally, what has come down to us today of their creations is far from what they imagined. Innumerable generations have added the diamonds they discovered as well as the dull metal which they mistook for gold. The transformation of the matriarchal society—in which myths were born—into a patriarchal society, the migrations, wars and invasions which impoverished or enriched the myths, all helped to transform them. In the animistic myths of the first ages, gods were already fermenting —the same gods who were later to put poetry into the straightjacket of religious dogmas. While it is true that poetry grows in the rich earth of magic, the pestilential miasmas of religion rise from the same ground and poison poetry—it must be set high above these noxious strata, if it is to regain its vigor.

The tribe of poets has little by little lost contact with the spirits of our fabulous totemic ancestors. They occupy such a high place in the skies that they now dominate the world where their first mumblings were heard, and have given to sorcerers and magicians the privilege of maintaining poetic contact with them. Mythical poetry, by becoming the exclusive possession of sorcerers, steadily got poorer and poorer until it was ossified into religious dogma. Thus, the most primitive tribes, those which have the least contact with occidental civilization and its religion and have the largest number of sorcerers, have myths of great poetic exuberance but few moral precepts. On the other hand, more evolved peoples see their myths lose their poetic brilliance even as their moral restrictions multiply! It's just as if morality were the enemy of poetry! Indeed, it is obvious that the absurd, not to say repugnant, morality of hypocrisy, vileness and cowardice which is prevalent in present-day society is not only the mortal enemy of poetry but of life itself! Conservative morality can only be the morality of the prison or of death.

Religion is "the illusion of a world which needs illusion," said Karl Marx. Certainly, if a world ever needed an illusion it is the one we live in! But is a perfectly harmonious world—one in which there would be no such need—conceivable? Such a world is just one more illusion: the horizon receding before our steps. El Dorado itself becomes indefinitely perfectible as soon as one lives in it. Tomorrow has advantages which we will always covet no matter how dazzling the present may seem. It does not necessarily follow that this illusion will take the form of religious dupery—that heavenly felicities will compensate for the wretched poverty of slave life. That sort of illusion belongs to the world of violence and horror whose inevitable end is at hand. The new world, which shows signs of coming into being, will set out to destroy hell on earth and replace it with the absolute heaven of religion, transformed into a more-or-less human paradise. Just as an infernal life requires heavenly consolation, so a more harmonious world than ours would give rise to an exalted and living illusion of life for the future generations which will perfect it. This collective illusion, which will remain forever unsatisfied, will thus constantly be renewed. The primitive myth, devoid of consolation and including only elementary taboos, is nothing but poetic exaltation. The reason is simple: in primitive tribes the division of work is such that there are no notable differences of status among the members. They form an almost completely homogenous group whose essential needs—there are not others!—are more or less satisfied. At the very least, some do not die of hunger while others burst with plenty!

As a society grows, it develops inequalities of condition. These are sanctioned, justified and emphasized by moral restrictions and law. The future world will seek to do away with these inequalities by applying the following principle: from each according to his means, to each according to his needs—and thus the necessity of a divinity which, in an illusory way, compensates for social inequality, will disappear. While religion will evaporate, the poetic myth, purified of its religious content, will be as necessary as ever. Religion still succeeds in carrying on today because it continues to satisfy—at five and ten cent rates—the need for the marvelous, a need which is deep in the heart of the masses.

Another modern phenomenon is the creation of atheistic myths, completely lacking in poetry and planned to nourish and direct the latent religious fanaticism of people who have lost contact with divinity but whose need for religious consolation persists. Thirty or forty centuries ago, the superhuman chief, quasi-deified during his lifetime, would have been elevated to some Olympus after his death—had he died at the height of his success. Doesn't Hitler say that he is "an ambassador of Providence," a sort of German Messiah? Doesn't Stalin take the title, "The Sun of the People"—which is more than the Inca who only thought of their leader as the son of the sun? Are not both Stalin and Hitler supposed to possess divine infallibility? These attempts to attribute divine qualities to mortal persons, who shine with glory and supernatural virtues, show how material conditions create the conditions for religious anguish, which, if not managed by religion proper, will be directed towards a leader.

"Poetry should be made by all—not by one." This injunction of Lautréamont will no doubt one day be heeded because poetry has already been the fruit of the active and passive collaboration of entire peoples. If primitive societies constitute the childhood of humanity—as is commonly admitted—the present-day world is its reformatory, its prison. But the doors of the prison will open and humanity will again find her perpetual youth at the prospect of liberty. The myths and legends of primitive people show the great liberty of their minds. So great in fact that few men will admit its greatness, most calling it delirium instead.

Such works may well seem behind us, no longer relevant for the dark underground region in which we live. But at the other end, the exit which we are approaching, there is light—light so blinding that we cannot yet distinguish the objects it illuminates and can scarcely imagine ourselves ever being in such splendor.

Primitive man does not yet know himself but seeks his identity. Modern man has lost his way. The man of tomorrow must first find himself, recognize himself and, contradictorily, become conscious of himself. He will have the means to do so. Perhaps he already has them, without being able to use them, because he is not free to think under present conditions. If the man of yesterday, who knew no limits to his thought but those imposed by his desire, was able, despite his struggle against Nature, to produce marvelous legends, what could not the man of tomorrow create—he who will be conscious of his own nature and will dominate the world more and more because his mind will be freed from all shackles?

Just as myths and legends are the collective poetic product of societies in which social inequalities were so slight that marked oppression could not come into existence, the collective practice of poetry is only conceivable in a world freed from all oppression—a world in which poetic thought will once again be as natural to man as seeing or sleeping. This will be the "universal progressive poetry" which Frederick Schlegel foresaw some 150 years ago. This poetic thought, developing without any restrictions, will create exalted myths—myths whose essence will be the marvelous, a quality which will no longer frighten thought as it does today. These myths will be devoid of religious consolation since there will be no need for that in a world whose object is the provocative and tempting chimera of unattainable perfection.

It should not be inferred, however, that all the people will directly participate in poetic creation. But, instead of it being the work of a few individuals, it will be the life and thought of vast groups of men animated by the spirit of the masses. The bond between the poets and the people, which has been broken for so many centuries, will be restored. Today society subjects the masses to a miserable existence which—as has already been mentioned—keeps them away from poetry. But the aspiration towards poetry remains latent in the masses. The popularity of stupidly sentimental literature, adventure novels, etc., reveals this need for poetry. In our days, poetry has become the almost exclusive attribute of a small number of individuals who are the only persons to realize—more or less clearly—its necessity.

Spurious poetry for the use of the masses is intended to satisfy their need for poetry and also to provide a safety valve to regulate their spiritual pressure. It offers them a sort of escape or consolation to make up for their burnt-out religious faith and it turns their desire for the irrational into harmless channels. Just as the masters think that religion is necessary for the people, they judge that authentic poetry is harmful to society, because it might help to emancipate the people. The masters are suspicious of the subversive nature of poetry. Therefore, they make every effort to stifle it and to an extent they have succeeded in creating an actual zone of silence around poetry in which it has become rarefied.

Finally, the constantly decreasing number of poets—fortunately, some still exist!—emphasizes this rupture between the poets and the masses and shows again that present-day society is suffering its death pangs. There is an analogy between our period and the end of feudal French society. Although the latter was marked by an expansion of philosophic thought, which created the intellectual basis for the gestating regime, it was also characterized by a dearth of poetry. There was not a single French poet worthy of the name in the 18th century. And those who called themselves poets were soon reduced by Romanticism to dust, settling on the sedan chairs and wigs forgotten in musty attics.

It was Romanticism that rediscovered the marvelous and gave it a revolutionary significance which it has kept to this day, and which has allowed it to live—like an outlaw, but to live, nevertheless. I say outlaw because the real poet cannot be recognized as such if he does not oppose the world in which he lives with complete nonconformism. He combats everyone, including the revolutionists who take a purely political viewpoint—which must necessarily be isolated from the cultural movement as a whole—and who advance the idea that culture should take a back seat to the attainment of the social revolution. There is not a single poet or artist, conscious of his place in society, who does not think that this urgently needed and indispensable revolution is the key to the future. However, the idea of submitting poetry and all culture dictatorially to a political movement seems to me as reactionary as to want to keep them separated from politics. The "ivory tower" and "proletarian art" are merely two sides of the same coin. While the reactionaries would like to make poetry the lay equivalent of religious prayer, the revolutionists are too apt to confuse it with publicity. The poet of today has no other choice than to be a revolutionist or not to be a poet, for he must constantly hurl himself into the unknown; the step he took yesterday in no way gets him off the hook for the one he will take tomorrow, since every day everything has to be begun all over again. Even what he acquired in sleep turns to ashes upon awakening. There is no secure movement. He should receive nothing, neither praise nor laurels, but he should give everything to the task of beating down the barricades of habit and routine—barricades which keep on rising.

Today he must be the "accursed" poet. This malediction cast at him by society indicates his revolutionary position; but he will come out of his enforced reserve and be placed at the head of society when it has been split from top to bottom, and when it will have recognized the common human origin of poetry and science. Then the poet, with the active and passive collaboration of the people, will create myths exalting the marvelous that will send the entire world out to assault the Unknown.

Translated by Libby Ginway

THE DISHONOR OF POETS

An Essay on Aragon and Eluard

Mexico, February 1945

The poetic works from the end of the last century that were considered the most hermetic or the most delirious are becoming clearer day by day. When most of the other works that offered no resistance to immediate comprehension have grown dim, when those voices through which large numbers of people were pleased to effortlessly recognize their own voices have been stilled, it is strikingly clear that these difficult works have contradictorily begun to speak for us. Their darkness, pierced in the beginning by a single phosphorescent point that only very experienced eyes could see, has been replaced by a light that we know one day will be total. It is now beyond question that surrealist works will share the same lot as all the previous works that are historically situated. The climate of Benjamin Péret's poetry or Max Ernst's painting will then be the very climate of life.

— André Breton

IF ONE SEARCHES for the original significance of poetry, today concealed behind the thousand tawdry ornaments of society, one realizes that it is the veritable breath of man, the source of all knowledge, and knowledge itself in its most immaculate aspect. The entire spiritual life of humanity since the beginning of its consciousness is condensed in poetry; in it the highest creations live and, since its soil remains forever fertile, it holds perpetually in reserve the colorless crystals and the harvests of tomorrow.

Tutelary divinity with a thousand faces, it is here called love, there freedom, and elsewhere science. It remains omnipotent; it rushes forth in the mythical tales of the Eskimo, blazes in a love letter, mows down the execution squad as this squad shoots the worker who breathes his last sigh of social revolution, and therefore of freedom; it sparkles in the discovery of the scholar; faints, anemic, as the most stupid productions make use of it; and its memory, a eulogy which would like to be funereal, still pierces the mummified words of the priest, its assassin, to whom the faithful listen because they seek it, blind and deaf, in the tomb of dogma where it is no more than a fallacious dust.

Throughout history, the enemies of poetry have been obsessed with submitting it to their immediate ends, to crushing it with their god, or, as they are today, to chaining it to the proclamations of the new brown or "red" divinity—the reddish brown of dried blood—even bloodier than the former. For them, life and culture are summed up in the opposition between useful and useless, it being understood that the useful takes the form of a pickaxe wielded for their benefit. For them, poetry is only a luxury of the rich, the aristocrat or the banker, and if it should want to make itself "useful" to the masses, it must resign itself to being an "applied," "decorative," "household" art, et cetera.

Instinctively, they feel that poetry is the fulcrum demanded by Archimedes, and fear that if it is overturned, the world might fall on top of them. Thus their ambition is to revile it, to take away from it all efficacy, all power to exalt, in order to give it the hypocritically consoling role of a sister of charity.

But the poet does not have to maintain for others an illusory hope, human or celestial, or appease others' spirits by inflating them with an unlimited confidence in a father or leader, against whom all criticism becomes sacrilege. Quite the contrary, it is for the poet to pronounce the forever sacrilegious words and permanent blasphemies. The poet struggles against all oppression: in the first place that of man by man, but also in the oppression of his thought by religious, philosophical, and social dogmas. He fights so that man may attain an ever more perfectible knowledge of himself and the universe. It does not follow that he desires to put poetry in the service of a political action, even a revolutionary one. But his very nature as a poet makes him a revolutionary who must fight on all fronts: on the ground of poetry with the means proper to it, and on the field of social action, without ever confounding the two fields of action, for fear of reestablishing the very confusion he fights against, and consequently ceasing to be a poet—that is to say, a revolutionary.

Wars such as those we are now undergoing are possible only during a period when all of the forces of regression merge. They signify, among other things, an arrest in cultural growth—culture in this period has ceased to check the forces of reaction. This fact is so clear as to require no elaboration. From the momentary defeat of culture flows, fatally, the triumphant spirit of reaction—a spirit that is manifested, in its highest incarnation, as religious obscurantism. This resurrection of God, of the fatherland and leader, also came about as a result of the extreme condition of peoples' minds—minds degraded by war and maintained in this degraded state by those who benefited from this condition.

Consequently, the intellectual fermentation produced by this situation, insofar as intellectuals are abandoning themselves to the current, remains entirely regressive, a negative coefficient. Its products remain reactionary, whether they are "poetry" of fascist or anti-fascist propaganda, or of religious exaltation. Aphrodisiacs of old men, they restore a fugitive vigor to society only to better ruin it. The "poets" of today participate in none of the creative thought of the revolutionaries from the Year II or from Russia in 1917, for example, nor do they participate in the creative thought of the mystics or heretics from the Middle Ages. They are destined to provoke only an artificial exaltation in the masses, whereas the revolutionaries and mystics were the product of a real and profound collective exaltation which their words expressed. Revolutionaries and mystics expressed the thought and the hope of a whole people, imbued with the same myth or animated with the same impulse, while the "poetry" of propaganda tends merely to restore a little bit of life to a myth in the midst of its death throes. As civic hymns, they have the same soporific virtues as the religious patrons, from whom they directly inherited the conservative function; for if mythical and then mystical poetry created the divinity, the hymn exploits this same divinity. Similarly, the revolutionary from the Year II or from 1917 created a new society—a society taken advantage of by the patriots and Stalinists today.

To illustrate what I have just stated, I need only refer to a small pamphlet published in Rio de Janeiro, *The Honor of Poets*, which contains a selection of poems published clandestinely in Paris during the Nazi occupation. Not one of these "poems" surpasses the lyrical level of pharmaceutical advertising, and it is not accidental that their authors, for the most part, believed they should return to rhyme and classical Alexandrines. Form and content necessarily keep the strictest rapport, and in these "verses" the one and the other react against each other in a frantic race to the bottom. It is indeed significant that most of these texts identify Christianity and nationalism with one another, as if they wanted to demonstrate that religious dogma and nationalist dogma have a common origin and an identical social function. Even the title of the pamphlet, *The Honor of Poets*, considered with respect to its content, assumes a direction foreign to all poetry. In short, the honor of these "poets" consists in ceasing to be poets in order to become publicity agents.

In the work of Loys Masson this alloy—religion-nationalism—contains a greater portion of fideism than patriotism. Accustomed to the Amens and the ecclesiastical power of Stalinism, Aragon does not, however, succeed as well as the aforementioned in uniting God and country. He recovers the first, I dare say, only tangentially, and obtains a text capable of making only one author turn green with envy—the author of the tiresome phrase on French radio: "Furniture by Levitan is guaranteed for a long time."

It was a time for suffering
When Jeanne came to Vaucouleurs
Ah! Cut France into pieces
Day had that pallor
I remain king of my sorrows.

But it was Paul Eluard who alone of all the authors in the pamphlet was a poet, and who wrote the most complete civic litany:

On my gourmand and tender dog
On his raised ears
On his clumsy paw
I write your name

On the springboard of my door
On the familiar objects
On the tide of blessed water
I write your name....

In reality, all the authors of this pamphlet, without admitting it, even to themselves, depart from and aggravate an error of Guillame Apollinaire. Apollinaire wanted to treat war as a subject for poetry. But if war, considered as combat and relieved of any nationalist spirit, can remain strictly speaking a poetic subject, it cannot be associated with a nationalist shibboleth, even if the nation in question, like France, was savagely oppressed by

110

the Nazis. The expulsion of the oppressor and the propaganda to that end, spring from political, social or military action, according to the manner in which the expulsion is envisaged. In any case, poetry does not have to intervene in the debate other than through its own action, through its own cultural significance, for poets are free to participate as much as revolutionaries in overthrowing the Nazi adversary, without ever forgetting that this oppression corresponded to the wishes, admitted or not, of all the enemies—first national, then foreign—of poetry, a cultural form that enables the total liberation of the human mind; for, to paraphrase Marx, poetry has no country since it exists in all times and all places.

There is still much to be said concerning freedom, a word so often evoked in these pages. First, what type of freedom are we talking about? Freedom for a small number to oppress the whole population, or the freedom for this population to bring the small number of the privileged to their senses? Freedom for believers to impose their god and morality on the whole society or freedom for the society to reject God, his philosophy, and his morality? Freedom is like "an inhalation of air," said André Breton, and in order to fulfill its role, this inhalation of air must first throw off the miasma of the past which infests this pamphlet. As long as the malevolent phantoms of religion and fatherland collide with the social and intellectual atmosphere, under whatever disguise they borrow, no freedom will be conceivable: their previous expulsion is one of the prime conditions for the advent of freedom.

Every "poem" which willfully exalts an indefinite "freedom," even when it is not embellished with religious or nationalist attributes, ceases first of all to be a poem and ultimately becomes an obstacle to the total liberation of man, for it deceives by indicating a "freedom" which merely conceals new chains.

On the other hand, from every authentic poem escapes a breath of complete and stirring freedom (even if this freedom is not evoked in its political or social aspect), and thus it contributes to the effective liberation of man.

(excerpts)
Translated by Cheryl Seaman

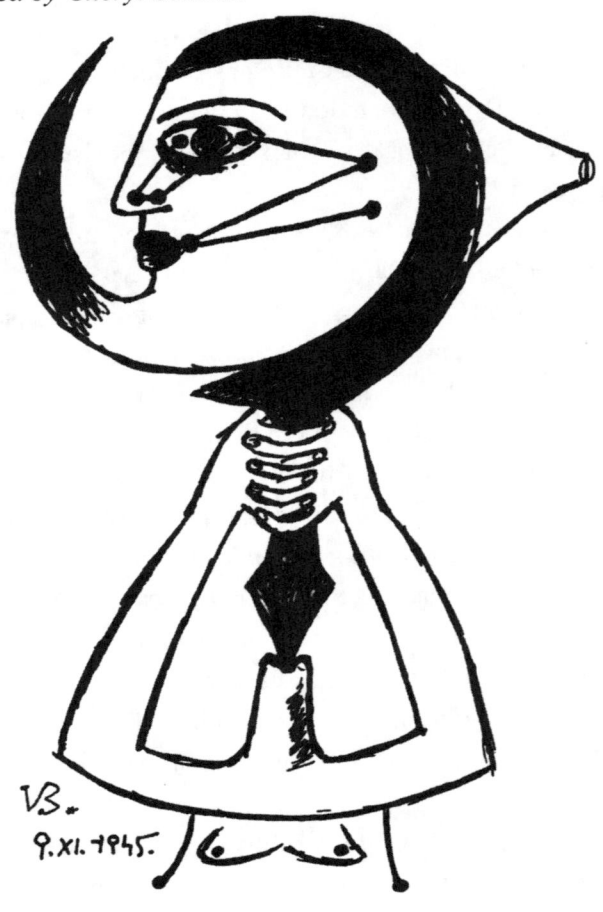

Victor Brauner: Drawing for *Main Forte*

THE FACTORY COMMITTEE: MOTOR OF
THE SOCIAL REVOLUTION

N O ONE WILL DENY that capitalist society has entered a period of permanent crisis—a crisis that induces it to reassemble its weakened forces and to concentrate, more and more, all political and economic power in the hands of the state, by means of nationalizations. Against this concentration of capitalist power, are we going to continue to oppose the scattered forces of the workers? To do so would be to run towards decisive defeat. And one of the principal reasons for the present apathy of the working class resides in the interminable series of defeats suffered by the social revolution throughout this century.

The working class no longer has confidence in any organization because it has observed them all at work, here and there, and seen that all of them, including the anarchist organizations, have revealed themselves incapable of resolving the crisis of capitalism—that is to say, of assuring the triumph of the social revolution. One must not be afraid to say that all of these organizations are outdated and no longer valid. On the contrary, only this very realization—the importance of which should not be downplayed by more or less circumstantial considerations, nor by blaming others for the consequences of one's own errors— provides a point of departure from which we can truly prepare ourselves to revise all doctrines (which today share a substantial portion of outdatedness), perhaps resulting in a fundamental ideological unification of the workers' movement in the direction of the social revolution. It goes without saying that I do not by any means dream of a movement whose thought would be monolithic, but a movement unified from within, and in which diverse tendencies would enjoy the freedom to manifest themselves fully.

On the other hand, it is no less true that action is called for immediately. This action must obey two general principles: first, it must facilitate the ideological regrouping mentioned above; and second, it must cease to consider the revolution as the work of future generations for whom we are supposed to make preparations. We are faced with this dilemma: either the social revolution and a new impetus for humanity, or war and a social decomposition concerning which the past offers only a few pale examples.

History is granting us a breathing space the duration of which we do not know. Let us make use of it to reverse the course of the present degeneration and to bring about the revolution. The present apathy of the working class is only temporary. It indicates, at this time, both the workers' loss of confidence in all organizations, and a certain detachment on their part. It depends on us, as revolutionaries, to draw the lessons which will enable this detachment to be transformed into active revolt. The energy of the working class asks only for an opportunity to exert itself. Nevertheless, it is necessary to give it not only an end—it has had a presentiment of this for a long time—but also a means of attaining this end. If the task of revolutionaries is to bring about a fraternal society, this requires the immediate formation of an organism in which this fraternity can form and develop itself.

At the present time it is on the factory level that workers' fraternity attains its highest level. Thus it is there that we must act, but not in clamoring for a trade-union unity which is chimerical today, in the actual conditions of the capitalist world, and which, moreover, could only come forward against the working class, since the trade unions now represent only different tendencies of capitalism. In fact, a "united front" of the unions could happen only on the eve of the revolution—and would act against the revolution since the major unions would all be equally interested in torpedoing it to assure their own survival in the capitalist state. Henceforth, as integral parts of the capitalist system, they defend this system by defending themselves. The interests of the union are essentially their own and not those of the workers.

Moreover, one of the most powerful obstacles to a workers' regrouping and a revolutionary renaissance is constituted by the apparatus of the union bureaucrats, even in the factory, beginning with the Stalinist apparatus. The enemy of the worker today is the union bureaucrat every bit as much as the boss who, without the union bureaucrat, would most of the time be powerless. It is the union bureaucrat who paralyzes workers' action. And thus the first watchword of revolutionaries must be: Out the door with the union bureaucrats!

But the principal enemy consists of Stalinism and its union apparatus, because they are the partisans of state capitalism— that is to say, the complete fusion of the state and unionism. They are therefore the most clear-sighted defenders of the capitalist system, since they outline, for this system, the most stable state conceivable today.

Meanwhile, one should not destroy an existing organism without proposing another in its place, better adapted to the necessities of the revolution. And it is precisely the revolution that has taken upon itself the task of showing us, each time that it has appeared, the instrument of its choice: the factory committee directly elected by the workers assembled on the shop-floor, with memberships that are revocable at any time. This is the only organism which is able, without alteration, to direct the workers' interests within the capitalist society while looking toward the social revolution; and which is also able to accomplish this revolution, and, upon attaining victory, constituting the basis of a future society. Its structure is the most democratic conceivable, since it is directly elected in the workplace by all the workers, who control its actions from day to day and who are able to recall a member of the committee, or the entire committee, at any time, and choose another. Its constitution offers the least risk of degeneration, because of the constant and direct control that the workers are able to exercise over their delegates.

Furthermore, the constant contact between elected and electors enables the highest possible degree of creative initiative on the part of the working class, which is thus called upon to take its destiny in its own hands and to directly lead its own struggles. This committee, which authentically represents the will of the workers, is called upon to administer the factory and to organize the workers' defense against the police and the reactionary gangs that work on behalf of Stalinism and traditional capitalism. After the victory of the revolution, the factory committee would indicate to the regional, national, and international leaders (these also are directly elected by the workers), the productive capacities of the factory and its needs in terms of raw materials and manpower. Finally, the representatives of each factory would be called to form, on the regional, national, and international scale, the new government, which would not be involved in the management of the economy, but whose principal task would be to liquidate the heritage of capitalism and to assure the material and cultural conditions of its own progressive disappearance.

At once economic and political, the factory committee is the revolutionary organism par excellence. That is why even its *establishment* represents a sort of insurrection against the capitalist state and its trade-union branches, because it assembles all the workers' energies against the capitalist state, and even assumes the latter's economic power. For this reason one sees it burst forth spontaneously in moments of acute social crisis. But in our epoch of chronic crisis, it is necessary for revolutionaries to passionately defend and advocate this form, starting now if they wish, in the first place, by working to put an end to the meddling of union bureaucrats in the factories, and to restore to the workers the initiative of their emancipation. Let us therefore destroy the unions in the name of the factory committees, democratically elected by all the workers in the plant, and revisable or revocable at any time.

Translated by Mary Low

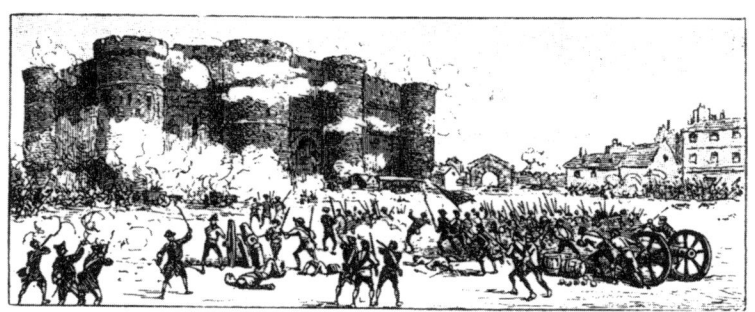

La prise de la Bastille.

POETRY ABOVE ALL

A Defense of Poetry

HARDLY A YEAR or even a month goes by without a protest arising against the ranking of art and poetry above science. First, someone praises the latest conclusions reached by psychology; then, someone else comes along who bases himself on the recent results of physics—it being well understood of course that he could only be referring to *nuclear* physics.

It so happens that reading such boorish humbug makes me shrug my shoulders. Moreover, I often make a vain effort to repress grating my teeth, especially when such opinions come from artists and poets. I know well that those who have already tested this illusion are legion, beginning with the futurists. But what remains of their manifestoes and most of the works which respond to this unreasonable demand?

To require the subordination of poetry and art to science is nothing but a redoubtable aberration, the denunciation of which must be pursued relentlessly since it consists in reversing the natural order of things, in which intuition fully precedes science. After all, the primacy of intuition and its ultimately determining character have been proclaimed, at least to some degree, even by those who scorn it, since they have not hesitated to give an atomic power station the name of Melusine—without the least concern over its noxious emanations, which threaten to dissolve its image, hitherto unaltered by poetry.

Nuclear fission and its consequences will never provoke a new mode of sensibility any more than they will engender original poetry. On the contrary, it is precisely the extreme agitation of the senses, initiated by Jean-Jacques Rousseau, that—via the

Revolution of 1789, romanticism and surrealism—has given birth to the scientific spirit, despite the well known perversion of the latter. Is it necessary to highlight, for the purpose of illustrating this point, the recent remark in the press to the effect that the rocket launched toward the moon departed from the very point that Jules Verne had chosen a hundred years earlier?

No, poetry and art cannot rely on science for their take-off. For an artist, it would be proof of a singular inferiority complex to recognize the right of the latter to guide the former. To do so would be, perhaps unconsciously, to deny, purely and simply, art and poetry, since they can no more prosper in a scientific climate than could a fish in the burning sands of the Sahara. Ultimately, both demand a total freedom, and both contribute to such a state. Science which, for its part, remains subject to strict disciplinary rules, can contribute to the liberation of man, but also to his enslavement. The invention of the atomic bomb proves this with such clarity that it is unnecessary to further press the point. But as long as science is not placed in the direct and immediate service of humanity, and at the same time is not directly employed against humanity, it is impossible to hold any confidence in its intentions.

And even if this were not so, there would still be no reason for accepting its tutelage, as is proposed by a so-called "Situationist International," which imagines itself to be the bearer of the new while fostering merely equivocation and confusion. But is it not in such troubled waters as these that one fishes for a situation?

Translated by Libby Ginway

THE THAW:

A Surrealist Tale

THE ROAD BORDERED by blue trees hid itself in a well. A fine rain of red wine fell on the cottony ground. A man advancing spinelessly with quilt-like steps, giving anyone who watched him a sensation of softness, rose out of a well onto a spongy road with a galaxy in his hair. As he approached, I noted with surprise that he did not have a galaxy on his head, but that his skull sweated stars, which flew up into the red air and exploded into white rays.

At the edge of the road a girl with eyes like a burning building looked out of the window of her house, which resembled a wooden shoe, and watched the man approach. Emotion animated her translucent face; from it emanated rainbow waves. She even seemed to be awaiting him. But it was not the case, and she left her window when the man was only a few steps from the shoe. He seemed to hesitate for a moment; then he rounded the tip of the shoe, and flowed like a cask of oil into a thicket of bottles surrounding the strange building, murmuring: "Leopardi! Leopardi!" in a heartrending tone. In the shoe's window appeared a delicate hand with a crystal nails, holding a blossoming almond tree, which gave off fitful spirals of splotched smoke. The almond tree fell on the cloudy road, where at once it took root, and a loud cry of surprise rang out inside the shoe: "Monaco! Oh my Monaco!"

The rain of red wine fell thick and fast; it hastened the coming of the blood-colored night. Black, winged forms, seemingly condensations of mist, moved heavily through the damp air, now and then giving off a brief phosphorescent bolt of lightning. The shoe seemed to house a strange, disquieting life; you didn't care to look it in the face for fear of becoming involved in it. Dull sounds of sacks falling on the beaten earth alternated with sharp sounds of broken window-panes and long drawn out, scarcely human sighs, which sounded like the slow tearing of heavy matter. Through the window that had remained open, the hand appeared for an occasional moment, shaking as if to punctuate a speech that could not be heard: but it alone was seen; the rest of the body remained invisible, either because it did not exist, or because the dense gloom prevailing inside the shoe hid it from sight.

Meanwhile heavy winged forms gathered above the house, surrounding it with great soft circles streaked by pale lightning blasts. Steadily the circles diminished, as if to fascinate the house. And indeed, the anxiety, the dire anguish clearly prevailing within, gave no doubt that this was the intent. An extreme agitation filled the house with a humming composed of varied sounds, dominated at times by a long, piercing shriek. Now and then the shoe gave way to a convulsive trembling; and innumerable black balls, the size of a fist, spurted from the roof to fall in a bundle on the ground, where they burst and mingled at once with the earth.

The trembling became progressively more frequent and more accentuated, the stream of black balls became denser, and at last the shoe seemed shaken in all directions by incessant shudders, so violent that it inevitably burst apart. So brutal, so violent and so complete was the collapse when it occurred, one wondered if it had really taken place. The earth trembled, and seemed to rise up like a milk-soup; a long somber flame with blue glints gushed beneath the shoe, which was hurled into the cavernous air, danced an instant in the flame, and burst like a wolf's bane blossom into moths, which darted madly in all directions, colliding with one another, and forming a mass so dense that the light, already diffuse like that given off by solar eclipses, grew darker still, becoming a shadowy dusk woven of dusty spider-webs.

Upon becoming accustomed to the reddish shadows, you could distinguish in place of the shoe a white human form, which you soon guessed to be a woman, her reclining body extended by her long blond hair. Her breathing like a killing machine, the spasms which shook her whole body (and which revealed long, perfect camellia branch-like legs), showed her to be alive. Suddenly a poisonous lightning bolt flashed through the thick layer of moths, and the woman vanished, covered over, absorbed by the great black forms whose wing-beats unleashed a heavy, damp tempest. Cries and moans pierced holes in the mass of wings, which became a sort of sieve, through which you could sometimes see an arm, a breast, or the bold gleam of hair.

Suddenly a new lightning bolt pierced the cloud of moths in the opposite direction, and the woman appeared, nude, her two arms raised towards the invisible heaven in a gesture of ecstasy, crying out at the top of her lungs: "I want all of life, all of life: Men, the birds who fly through flowery clouds, the flowers which simulate wild beasts like the beating of an outraged heart, the sea which can be held in its entirety in the palm of a hand, and the sulfurous night which is summed up in one drop or mortal perfume, gliding like a delirious locomotive over the rains of my veins, paying no heed to the thousand signals of my nerves. I want all of life for I am the whole world, all nature, even down to the stones which sparkle in the inviolable coffers of the toneless mountains."

Then the day reappeared, bursting forth in a forest of flames. The cloud of moths vanished, dissolved like a pinch of sugar in a glass of clear water, and came to rest, like drops of milky dew, on the body of the motionless woman, mute as a buried city which suddenly reappears in the daylight, invaded by bevies of sparrows. Thus was the woman. A honey-suckle vine, gliding along her legs, began to wind a long flowery shoot about her, and a little bird made a nesting place in her dense hair.

A multitude of stars of every color gleamed in the soft air, like the light cast by fish as they leap out of sunny water. Still motionless in her ecstatic pose, the nude woman was visibly undergoing a change. The veins of her arms, her temples, her whole body were rapidly turning a tender green, while her skin assumed the transparent hue of opal; soon it was clear that she was dead, that there remained of her nothing but a light envelope, like a soap bubble. And this empty form began to move slowly, with a solemn step, barely touching the grass which became discolored beneath her steps, leaving behind her a wake of heavy shadows, like those which are cast by the flight of bats at nightfall.

She quickly reached the road, where the birds were shedding their multicolored plumage to make for her a path of glory. And yet the shadow deepened behind her shoulders, giving her two half-open wings, infinitely extended. This shadow, growing denser and denser, was peopled with impalpable forms, moving, changing, and seeming to absorb one another. You had hardly distinguished a gigantic lion's head when the head unfolded, burst into bloom, and became an orchid, a hundred-fold larger than nature. The orchid in turn moved, broke into pieces, and became a windmill. The windmill liquefied, and from the black pool of shadow rose a Hindu divinity with a thousand flaming eyes, like a machine-gun firing in the night. The eyes blinked and went out, and were replaced with telegraph-wires along which you could see telegrams running. There were strange ones among them: "The black poppy invades the bridal gown. Where are the swallow's beaks?" Simple ones: "First thing tomorrow, color the bread." Sinister ones: "The blood is stirred." And many more which filed by, jostling one another, hurrying each other in the hopes of arriving first. But the telegrams became rapidly illegible, and the wires mingled with a great head of hair, upon which a radiant diadem shone forth.

And the woman, or rather, her transparent phantom, kept advancing toward a gilded lake, which gleamed in the distance like the eye of a wild beast in a shadowy corpse. Ahead of her, everything crystallized, lost its volume and melted into Rupert's drops, which condensed behind her neck into heavy, soft, intertwined shadows. But in the distance, far behind her, bright spangles glittered.

A crayfish stopped the stone that was rolling in the torrent, and covered it with a long gray veil.

Translated by Alice Mayoux

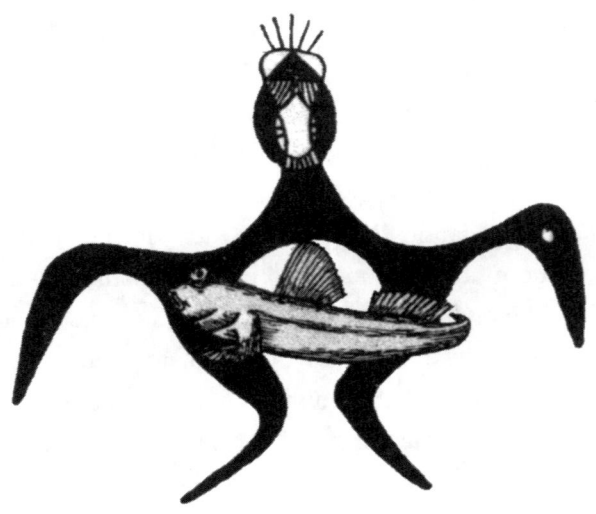

Collage/drawing from *Néon* illustrating the Gallant Sheep

THE GALLANT SHEEP

HONEY WITHOUT MOON, what have you done with my foot and the remains that were agitating convulsively under the thrust of their passions?

It was a beautiful day when the sea withdrew to let pass a white automobile in which slept a skin covered with lice. The automobile ran at a speed one could calculate while cutting an apple in quarters. It was equal to the trail of salt that the automobile left behind. White automobile, you grow in the distance. You occupy the whole visual field that my eyes can run during an entire year and your chauffeur, whose desire to not establish contact between the sea and your wheels I have not seen till now, salutes me. He is tall. He has an eye between his legs. His head oscillates on his shoulders like the balance of a pendulum. The needle marks 5 o'clock on the surface of the sea. Suddenly, the auto stops and the man at the head of the pendulum rushes up to meet me. He has steps of light and gestures of precaution. Everything in him is physical and blue, as far as his respiration, which diffuses around him a sky of spring mornings, making the swallows hesitate to leave the country. He is now four yards in front of me. His legs are spread apart and he sucks up the sun avidly.

"It's science," he murmurs. And the shadow of the Shepherd issues from the depths of his pants. For a long time, it follows a fly that has taken off at the mention of science.

The man rises. The sun's needle projects its shadow on his face in the form of a shoe sole covered with nails. I recognize Nestor who hourly dances waltzes under the sun. The sun imitates him and the shadows follow the movement. Go, then, after what entrusts you to the sun-dial. Nestor looks at me and recognizes that I am his friend. He tells me his hopes and his grief that are like the algae of mirrors:

"I am alone, it is true, but to well-born souls the cross does not count upon the number of diamonds. One day I was in a barn with straw and cows. The cows ate the straw and vice versa; although that must seem strange to you. And yet what happened to me next is perhaps even stranger yet. I was looking with the delight suitable to this sort of spectacle, the cows eating the straw, when the roof split, the whole length of the barn. A white sheet passed through the opening and flapped at a breath of wind that I did not feel at all. Then, slowly, it descended to the ground. The ground, in turn, opened. And I saw, following a rigorously perpendicular line, a little red fish descend from the roof by gliding along the sheet, and bury itself in the earth. It was followed by a second, then a third. Finally the number grew as rapidly as their dimension and the rarefaction of the air in the upper strata of the atmosphere permitted. The wind swelled and the barn slipped away from the earth. When I say slipped away … it took off, or rather fled, for the barn was divided in two. One half left with the straw and the other with the cows and each in a different direction, coming to an end in the same place: the mountain of rabbit skins."

(excerpt)
Translated by Alice Mayoux

PORTRAIT OF SAINT-POL-ROUX

The sun withdraws from the mitres and casques
driven by the anger of forests
sweeping with its shadow
faces blackened with the soot of their dreams

like stairways
their dreams simulate nights and days
absurd like a pin at the summit of Kilimanjaro.

Alone on the stale snow
A man with eyes like planets
raised his arms, burdened with lilies
toward a marble sky
where eyes were raining
so beautiful that revolvers crackled.

A true marriage sky of marriage
where the bride, naked like the sea
waited for the man to throw down his lilies
replacing the echo
that trembled at the sound of his voice.

Translated by Cheryl Seaman

WITHOUT TOMATOES; NO ARTICHOKES

My tomatoes are riper than your wooden shoes
And your artichokes resemble my girl

At the market place
there was a tomato and an artichoke
and both were dancing round a turnip
who turned on the root

Dance tomato, dance artichoke
your wedding day will be clear as the gaze
of carps
The wooden shoes contemplate us
while crying tears of overripe pears
and when they sing they make a noise from the grave
which explodes and brings forth a corpse
The corpse beats his hands like a pebble on a
window pane
and says
No you will not have my tomato at that price

Translated by Cheryl Seaman

BLACK AND WHITE IN BRAZIL
Slave Uprisings in Brazil

I f there is any country that can be said to owe its economic existence to the African, that country is Brazil. This is so true that any account of the African in Brazil would be no less than the history of the country itself.

As early as the second half of the 17th century we find the first importations of "ebony" from the Gold Coast, Ivory Coast, Dahomey, Nigeria, Angola, etc., to supplement an Indian population that was insubordinate, difficult to capture, and harder yet to maintain in slavery.

From then till the abolition of slavery in 1889—that is to say, in the space of three centuries—no fewer than 30 million blacks, according to the most moderate estimates of Brazilian historians, were shipped to Brazil; and this represents only a small proportion of the total number of blacks sent to Bahia, which was the capital of the country and its chief port. These same historians describe how the slave-ships left Africa, laboring under their loads of Negroes who were packed together in the holds like slabs of meat in the modern refrigerators of Buenos Aires. Receiving just the bare minimum of food and water calculated to keep them alive; they were allowed on deck only once a day, when the dead were thrown overboard. This daily act of hygiene was the only one indulged in throughout the voyage. Suicides and epidemics were so frequent that it was no rare occurrence for a ship to arrive empty at Bahia. And even the few survivors were in such a condition at the end of the voyage that they were incapable of work for a couple of months. Then they were sold in the slave-markets, usually to sugar and tobacco planters, who more or less monopolized the entire productive activity of the country. Working from dawn to dusk under the supervision of a *feitor*—a kind of warder whose duties were as onerous as those of the gangsmen in the monstrous convict-settlements of Guiana, mainly consisting of flogging the workers into a frenzy of industry—they were then shut up for the night in the *senzala*, where the majority slept in chains.

Underfed, treated worse than the beasts of burden whose role they occupied, separated from their children, who according to the slave-code belonged to the boss and were sold as soon as they attained a marketable value, was it surprising that they deserted and rebelled?

Desertion was always very frequent, so much so that it became necessary to establish a special body of police to round up the fugitives. This force was under the command of *capitâes do matto* (captains of the forest), whose cruelty is still remembered in Brazil, and who preferred to kill fugitives rather than take the trouble to capture them alive. In the sanctuary of the virgin forest the escaped Negroes formed themselves into societies called *quilombos,* whose members usually had to take an oath never to surrender, under pain of being excluded from all *quilombos* in the future, and sometimes even under the pain of death. The regional histories of Brazil contain innumerable references to these *quilombos.* But the most important of all was that of Palmares, in the present State of Pernambuco, which numbered several millions of black fugitives, and whose history, on account of its similarity to the rebellion of Spartacus, is worth recording.

The Palmares *quilombo* seems to have been founded shortly after the expulsion of the Dutch from Pernambuco, a province they had occupied during the second third of the 17th century. This *quilombo*, having driven off the Portuguese on several occasions, soon acquired great prestige among the slaves of the district, who became eager to escape and throw in their lot with the Palmares *quilombo*, especially after it became known that most of the other *quilombos* had flocked to its standard.

The members of this *quilombo* had constituted themselves as a republic under the political and religious leadership of a *Zumbi* or *N'Zumbi* (Bantu for leader). But as was typical, this leader enjoyed no special prerogative, and was called upon only when a situation requiring organized action arose—for example, on the occasion of battles and religious festivals. There was no such thing as private ownership. The crops and all that was brought in from fishing and hunting belonged to the society. What little we know of their domestic organization leads us to suppose that the women were the wives of all and sundry; but since they were fewer than the men it is probable that their family life was based on some hybrid convention involving both group marriage and polyandry.

The Palmares *quilombo* maintained itself for twenty years, increasing in numbers throughout this period. A regular army was needed to reduce it to submission. The blacks of Palmares struggled on to the bitter end, and many, following the example of their *Zumbi,* committed suicide rather than surrender. Only a few hundred escaped with their lives and these were brought back into slavery.

Slave uprisings on the plantations were also very frequent, but were usually isolated to the location where the outbreak occurred, on account of the difficulty of establishing communication between different plantations, which were often separated by long distances. The first major recorded risings are those of Bahia and Minas Geraes, at the end of the 18th century. They were of course ruthlessly suppressed. Then there were a whole series of risings from 1800 to 1835, all in Bahia, with the exception of two: one, not very important, in Rio de Janeiro, the other in the State of Maranhão. But this latter was not, as the others were, confined to the slaves alone. It was rather a kind of Brazilian *jacquerie* in which whites, Indians, Negroes and racially mixed groups of every description joined forces against the Portuguese oppressor.

Of all the slave uprisings in Bahia the last was the most important, and the only one which included a complete program of political and social redress. The black Muslims were the force behind all these risings: the Hausas at first, and then the Nagos. Strictly speaking, the Nagos were not pure black Muslims like the Hausas, but blacks who had come under Islamic influence and had partially adopted the religion. The Nagos' ethnic characteristics are less clearly defined than those of the Hausas, who, before the European invasion, formed a clearly-defined group living on the banks of the middle Niger, in the present English colony of Nigeria; whereas the Nagos are still to be found in the region of Lagos, Porto-Novo, etc. Their language is used as an auxiliary language by all the people of the region, including the Hausas, from the Niger to the Ivory Coast. Thus in Brazil it was customary to label as Nago every slave who spoke this language, irrespective of whether it was his native tongue or the "Esperanto" that enabled him to communicate with the bulk of the other slaves.

During the night of January 6-7, 1835, the rising broke out simultaneously at different points of the town of Bahia. The insurgents, armed with pikes, axes, spades and mattocks, tried to rush the arsenal. Unfortunately the movement had been betrayed, and instead of the small guard they expected to find they were met with heavy fire. By dawn the rising had been extinguished. In the course of the subsequent investigation the ringleaders admitted that they had planned to massacre all the authorities as well as any others that might oppose their determination to set up a Negro republic. This was the last rising of slaves in Brazil.

A prosperous future now seemed in store for slavery, protected as it was by the existing laws and sanctioned by the moral authority of a despicable catholic church always ready to consecrate whatever forms of extortion are most likely to fill her coffers. Yet already there were signs of a movement to abolish slavery. In 1817 a revolution, or rather, a conspiracy, took shape in Pernambuco for the establishment of an independent republic to be known as the "Confederation of the Equator," separated from the Portuguese metropolis. This future republic proposed to do away with slavery. But the plot was discovered before the conspirators were in a position to execute their project.

* * *

The history of Brazil, and of the abolition of slavery at the end of the war, contains scarcely any trace of labor agitation. This may be ascribed to the rudimentary organization of pre-war industry, and, as a consequence of this, to the very weak class-consciousness of the Brazilian proletariat.

Only one popular rising is worthy of mention throughout this period, namely, the mutiny aboard the men-of-war, which were largely manned by Negroes. This mutiny was provoked by the abuse faced by the sailors. The least breach of discipline was punished by hundreds of strokes of the cat. The crews of two of the most powerful ironclads then in existence formed themselves into a "committee of action" and issued a manifesto calling on the men to mutiny. The rising broke out on November 22, 1910. A Negro, João Candido Felisberto, was elected leader, and was assisted by a staff, also voted upon by the crews, which contained no man of higher grade than second mate. The officers were thrown out and those that resisted, executed. The mutineers then informed the government that they would bombard the town of Rio de Janeiro, in whose harbor the ships lay at anchor, if they were not guaranteed a general amnesty and the abolition of corporal punishment. The government had no choice but to capitulate. But a fortnight later, when the ships had been disarmed, the government forced a second rising and was thus able to arrest all the ringleaders of the first. More than a thousand sailors were deported to the forests, and perished there. The ringleaders were subjected to an inquisition of torture and confinement which lasted two years, until finally the few survivors were summoned before a court-martial and acquitted, just at the moment when the government, having nothing more to fear, was pleased to pardon them.

Yet their sacrifice had not been in vain, for corporal punishment disappeared from that day forward.

* * *

The revolutionary crisis that broke upon the world in 1917 had is repercussions in Brazil, where a number of serious strikes broke out, becoming more and more frequent and intensive till they culminated in the general strike of 1919, which paralyzed the entire economic activity of the two most important centers in Brazil: Rio de Janeiro and São Paolo. In 1920, the movement receded.

In these strikes, as in the naval mutiny of 1910, the revolutionary element was not recruited, as in the previous century, from a single race, but from a class composed of a mixture of races. Whites, blacks and mixed groups were united in opposing the common enemy, rightly identified in the mind of the Brazilian proletariat with the boss. And since the latter was usually a foreigner, the lower middle-class, growing in numbers and impatient to take a more active part in state affairs, opened a campaign against foreign capitalists, denouncing them to the proletariat as the agents of Anglo-American imperialism, all the while neglecting to mention that the national capitalist economy was entirely subservient to the economic systems of Europe and the U.S.A. The 50 milliards of francs of foreign capital invested in Brazil testify to this state of dependency better than any other argument. The illiteracy of the masses enabled this nationalist undertaking, which succeeded in diverting the indignation of the masses against foreign capital and thus in safeguarding the interests of the national bourgeoisie. This is at the foundation of all the middle-class "anti-imperialist" agitation in Latin America in recent years, an agitation whose only effect can be to affirm the ascendancy of foreign capital, unless the proletariat intervenes, as it did in Chile, determined to enforce a resolutely Communist program.

(excerpted from "Black and White in Brazil")
Translated by Samuel Beckett

With him, the revolutionary movement has lost, September 1959, one of the very rare creative spirits who have, during an entire life, refused to convert their breath into money, or Goncourt or Stalin Prizes, or cocktails at Gallimard. Péret will remain for us an example, because he has defended his ideas not only in some exceptional circumstances, but day after day for forty years, by his refusal, renewed daily, to accept the least compromise with bourgeois or stalinist infamy.
 — *Socialisme ou Barbarie*

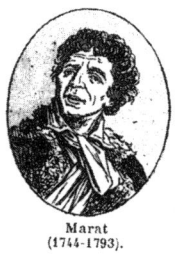

Marat
(1744-1793).

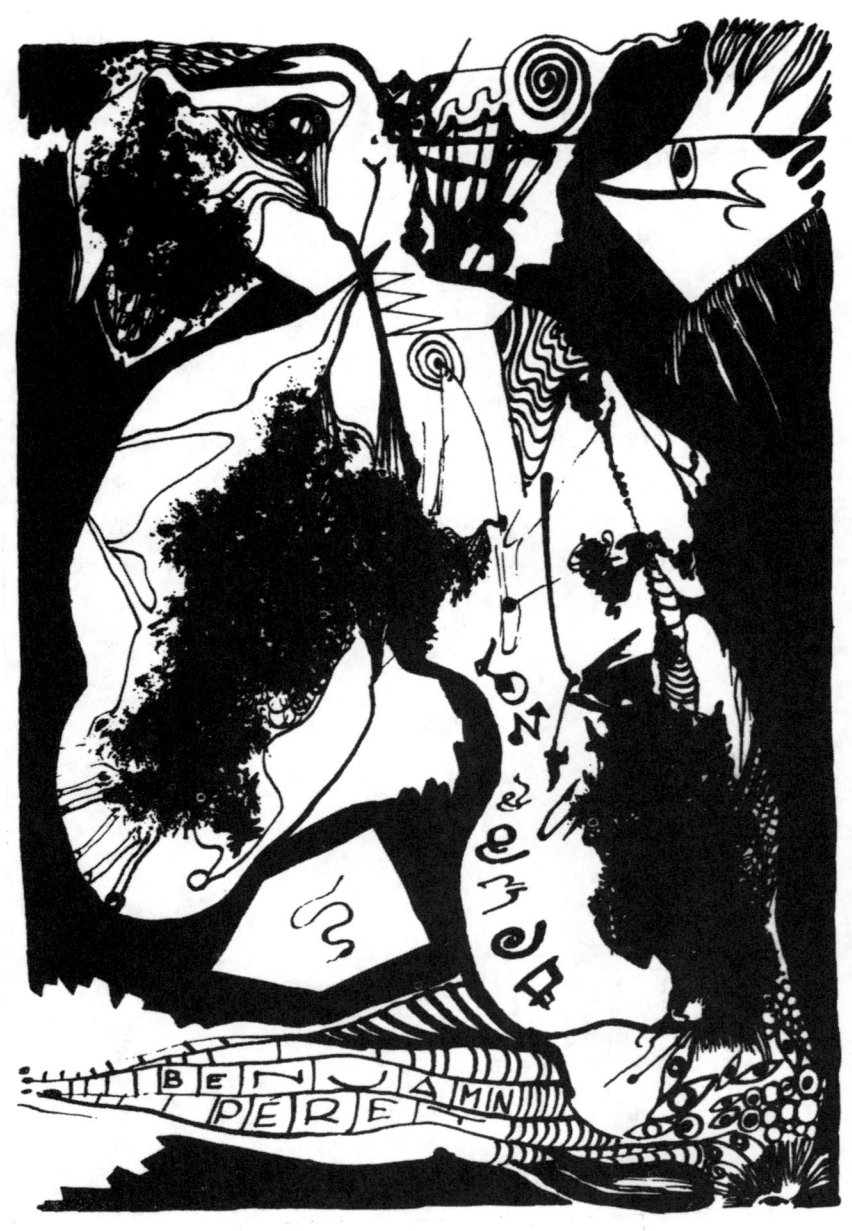

Schlecter Duvall: Homage to Péret

BENJAMIN PERET & THE ECOLOGICAL IMAGINATION

Don LaCoss

Thumbing through the journals and newspapers of the North American radical environmentalist movement, one is struck by how barren those pages are of poetry. This does not mean that there is no creative verse—on the contrary, there are plenty of paeans to sunrises over scruffy grasslands and quasi-transcendental contemplations on tree-sitting. I don't mean to put that kind of work down—we've all tried our hands at it at one time or another, and more people should be encouraged to try it, since there is a undoubtedly a useful function and a place for such creative output within the movement. But poetry is something a little bit different than rhyming couplets, and that difference is important. With this in mind, I urge those who believe in a staunch ecological stance that subverts the dominant patterns of objectification, degradation, subordination, and commodification to take the time to understand the revolutionary force of poetry.

Among those who can help in this regard are the surrealists. When one scrapes below the surface definitions of surrealism provided by universities, museums, and art dealers, one can begin to access the insurrectionary thirst for liberty that is the core of all for which surrealism fights—Dalí and Magritte, for example, are actually very marginal figures who were ejected from the movement for their reactionary views (it's probably no coincidence that, for those living in the US, Dalí and Magritte are the two most commonly marketed as surrealists). The fact of the matter is that the surrealism is *something else*—it's not an escape from reality, but a desperate bid to recover social realities in all their intensity and then transform them into deeper, higher, and *more real* levels of reality. This is accomplished by delivering the means of production (material and mental) into the hands of persons most exploited by the conventions of consensual reality built and maintained by the white, patriarchal, Christian bourgeoisie who have robbed people of their ability to imagine alternatives and wild possibilities by denigrating perception, desire, instinct, and intuition.

To combat the poisonously narrow and limiting conditions of modern life under capitalism, the surrealists braided together the complexities of individual revolt and the handsomely many-headed beast of collective rebellion. They believed that any revolution for social justice is doomed to failure if it does not allow for the unthinkable and indescribably unanticipated models of emancipation that poetry propagates—poetry and revolution are more than terms of balance, they are as intimately integral to one another as wind and rain. Poetry wrings out the repression that saturates our words and phrases by turning them inside out and knotting to them together into stormy new topological geometries. It is language at its most evolved and most primordial state, beyond and before the blinders of ideological policing and economic determinism; like the natural world, poetry is restlessly animate and sublimely turbulent, a riot of energies, colors, sounds and realities that scream out alternatives to the standard concepts and presuppositions of our scientific, ethical, and aesthetic vocabularies. One of the most militant of the surrealist poets was Benjamin Péret; in 1945, he wrote articulately about how poetry serves the revolution only when the revolution serves poetry:

> The poet battles against all oppression: primarily, that of one
> being over another, as well as the oppression of the mind by

religious, philosophical and social dogma. The poet struggles so that humanity may achieve a more perfect knowledge of itself and its world. This does not conform to the idea that poets put poetry at the service of political action, however revolutionary it might be. Just by being a poet, one becomes a revolutionary who must fight on all planes, both on the field of poetry by the most appropriate means and on the field of social action, without confusing the two terrains of action. To do so would be to risk a restoration of confusion that is meant to be dissipated, and by this one would cease to be a poet, or which is to say, a revolutionary.[1]

Apropos of my comments about poetry and radical ecology, I want to call attention to an overlooked collection of essays by Benjamin Péret called Natural History (originally, *Histoire naturelle*[2]). Falling somewhere between poetry, cosmogony, and mythology, Péret's *Natural History* is not only an important contribution to surrealism's thinking on the revolutionary restoration, emancipation and recreation of wildness and wilderness, but it also can be read as an experiment in radical environmentalist poetry that provides an interesting counterpoint and complement to so many of the other texts of radical ecology being passed around today—perhaps it is time for some eco-anarchist publications to re-run excerpts of it.

* * *

First, though, a few words on Benjamin Péret: one of the most pivotal, pioneering personalities in surrealism before and after World War II, Péret spent at least forty years of his life working with anti-state communists and anarchosyndicalists around the world. Motivated by protests against imperialist wars in North Africa, Péret joined the French Communist Party around 1926; by 1927, he was living in Brazil and helped organize an "oppositionist" (anti-Stalinist) communist league in Rio de Janeiro, but was soon imprisoned and deported back to France by Brazilian authorities for his revolutionary activities in 1932. In Paris, he bounced between small, anti-Stalinist communist organizations before signing on to the Internationalist Workers Party in 1936. During the revolution in Spain, he worked as a go-between for Trotskyist, far-left communist, and anarchosyndicalist militias in France, Brazil, Spain, and Mexico. An unrepentant antimilitarist and anticlericalist (there's a famous 1926 photograph of Péret spitting either insults or mucus at a priest), he also served in the Amigos des Durutti militia on the Aragon Front to fight against fascists, counter-revolutionaries, and Stalinists in 1937.

With the victory of Franco's clerico-fascist regime, Péret returned to France, and when the Nazis invaded, he was drafted by the French army to work as a clerk in a municipal office in Nantes. Unbelievably, his job allowed him access to lists of politically "suspicious" persons being compiled by the police, so he spent his time substituting the names of priests for those of subversives on the intelligence reports and clandestinely building up a Trotskyist cell, which was later broken up by the police and resulted in his incarceration.

After bribing his way past Nazi prison guards, Péret returned undercover to Occupied Paris, but was denounced as a threat to public safety by a local collaborationist newspaper, so he escaped to Marseilles and combined forces with the antifascist underground there before making it into exile to New York City. US authorities refused to issue him and his companion Remedios Varo visas because of their revolutionary political pasts, and so the couple went on to Mexico, where they hitched up with a community of exiled Spanish Trotskyists and civil war veterans. There, working alongside Natalia Sedova (Trotsky's second wife and comrade) and Grandizo Munis (formerly of the left-opposition Leninists in Spain and a veteran of the Amigos des Durutti), Péret produced bulletins critical of the Fourth International's theoretical and bureaucratic direction, before finally leaving the International himself in the summer of 1947 after it formally endorsed Stalin's USSR.

Péret worked within a number of ultra-left groups in Paris made up of anti-Stalinist veterans of the Spanish Civil War, Mexican anarchocommunists, and radical Vietnamese anti-imperialists—one of these groups was the International Workers Union, an organization aligned to the "Gallienne-Pennetier tendency" of Trotskyism whose membership included Munis, Jean Malaquais, Sania Gontarbert, Marcel Pennetier, and Serge Bricianer. He also wrote columns and signed surrealist proclamations that appeared in the largest of the dozen or so major anarchist newspapers produced in France at the time. Péret toyed with ideas on autonomist Marxism, council communism and a number of other left-communist internationalist undertakings in brochures and newspaper columns until his death in 1959.[3] In a glowing eulogy, the revolutionary direct democracy "Socialisme ou barbarie" group hailed him as one of the "very rare creative spirits" who "defended his ideas" daily and continually renewed "his refusal to accept the least compromise with bourgeois or Stalinist infamy." Yet in spite of this, his uncompromising ideas and creations remain largely unexplored by contemporary practitioners of radical theory, including his oddly beautiful "natural history" written between 1945 and 1958.

* * *

To reappraise Péret's *Natural History* as a text of surrealist ecology, one can begin by reflecting upon the attributes and meaning of "natural history" itself as a discipline of study. In these days of university -ologies (biology, zoology, climatology, paleontology, physical anthropology), the term *histoire naturelle* is old-fashioned, almost pre-scientific (in the most modern sense of the word "science")— in other words, pre-industrial, pre-capitalist, and lo-tech in its gadgetry. Whereas scientists today will not form a hypothesis for controlled experiments without funding from a major corporation, natural historians since the Roman writer Pliny the Elder tended to be obsessed amateurs skilled in the art of observation who tirelessly detailed even the most obvious elements of the world around them with great care. Thus, at least ideally, natural history has come to be understood as a systematic consideration of animal, vegetable, and mineral phenomena based on close, but detached, observation by the writer (Pliny, for example, died while investigating first-hand the volcano eruption at Pompeii in 79 CE). The empirical and materialistic study of natural history covered all forms of organic and inorganic existence: stars, planets, plants, minerals, fossil remains, birds, mammals, and insects were all fair game.

Natural history changed considerably in the mid-1700s thanks to the aristocratic sycophant Count Georges-Louis Leclerc Buffon, who produced a sprawling forty-four volume *Histoire naturelle, générale et particulière* (1749-88). Buffon's buffoonery quickly earned him an esteemed place among the snooty firmament of the European Enlightenment, and most twentieth-century schoolchildren in France—even a dropout underachiever like Péret—would have had at least a little of his work shoved down their throats. Buffon's studies are of value insofar as they discussed descent with modification and mentioned causative influences present in environments, including migration patterns, geography, and population density, thereby providing a vital cornerstone for evolutionists such as Darwin to build upon later. Regrettably, though, Buffon curdles these innovations by adding his own loathsome inflections to the eighteenth-century debates on "race." The only real use in mentioning Buffon here is to juxtapose his version of natural history to the essays that make up Péret's: whereas Buffon provides anemic, mechanistic, and reasonably dull explanations for life and nature through carefully-detailed accounts and sharply realistic illustrations, Péret's texts are fiery and funny, playfully satirizing the sometimes pretentious conventions of the "natural historian" genre in very deliberate ways.

Péret's assembled essays, "The Four Elements," "The Mineral Kingdom," "The Vegetable Kingdom," and "The Animal Kingdom," demonstrate an unremarkable taxonomic scheme as far as natural histories go, but one that diverges sharply from any other from its opening lines which describe the world as "not spherical but shaped like a bowl, and is one of the breasts of heaven. The other is to be found at the center of the Milky Way." This natural history rings more like the popular myths, legends, and folk tales of Mesoamerica that Péret anthologized, or episodes from the ancient Yucatan Jaguar Prophet that appear in the *Book of Chilám Balám* that Péret translated in 1955. In fact, much of the action in *Natural History* seems pregnant with portent, like the encoded allegorical formulae of medieval alchemical treatises that synthesized philosophy, chemistry, and physics in the service of radical moral change. One need only be a skilled adept to decipher its recipe.

Divided further into "Earth," "Air," "Water," "Fire" subsections, "Four Elements" spells out the most unnatural explanations and recountings of these allegedly foundational building blocks of nature. Air, Péret explains, secretes pepper that accumulates in the upper atmosphere to give stars their sparkle; evaporated sea water leaves behind female silks that, after one thousand years of maturation, produce four litters of brandy glasses a year; and damp, trembling stones exposed to sunlight yield "soft, sweet, velvety and perfumed" fire "currently used for burning down churches." Water, air, earth and fire combined to create the world in "The Mineral Kingdom." But rather than the graceful ideals of classical legend, Péret's elements are capricious, vain, and rambunctious, brawling with one another like demonic Three Stooges. The tumult of "The Vegetable Kingdom" is related with the same cruel charm: "Disorder reigned under the cover of the night. The honeysuckle came from nowhere zigzagging to escape a pine that was tilting at it and threatening to impale it. A pansy was sitting astride a heliotrope pulling out its hair in handfuls. The whole place was an appalling free-for-all, an incredible orgy."

The last chapter, "The Animal Kingdom," the final evolutionary stage in Péret's creation myth, is not only a wicked inversion of the Book of Genesis, but it is also a radical assertion that nature exists for its own sake well outside of the needs and largesse of humans. It opens with a scene of havoc described as disgusting, so much so that the agave takes it upon itself to relieve the misery and does so by accidentally creating an anteater, a grasshopper, a cod, and a woodpecker. Each time a new creature appears, the agave (a significant plant in Mexican culture, not the least of which is as a central ingredient in the making of tequila) reacts with surprise and delight, a far cry from the self-centered braggart in Genesis who wills things into existence with nothing but humorless ostentation.

In fact, Péret mocks the anthropocentrism of the Judeo-Christian god when he provides all-too-human qualities to the agave: while soaking a giraffe in grease in order to make "a sparrow or a frigate bird," the agave bends down to retie its footwear and snaps a shoelace, the discarded useless end of which transforms into a dog-producing primrose bush. The agave also manipulates grammatical, philosophical, scientific and literary concepts during its paroxysms of creation: sophisms, alexandrines, synonyms, prepositions, Archimedes' principle, and circumflex accents combine with panthers, pelicans, pinecones, and rhinoceroses. During a fight and yelling match between a starfish, a mouse, and a heron, the agave finally decides to create a man, carving him from a prune and telling him to find a wife on his own, which the prune-man attempts with honey from a hive.

My flat synopsis does nothing to capture the wonder, humor, and rebellious zest of Péret's *Natural History*, but it does help to show how the essays could be approached as foundational text of a radical ecological agenda. Péret's casting of his essays under the rubric of "kingdoms" is a farcical swipe at the classification system of eighteenth-century botanist Carolus Linnaeus, the creator of the orderly rigid network of organizational principles used by humans to identify and record plant and animal life. In contrast to the self-serving human urge to force order upon the world—the very notion of a "natural history" is supremely conceited in assuming that nature can be squeezed into a human-forged narrative of change over time—the kingdoms imagined by Péret are unruly and regicidal, ungoverned and ungovernable save for a chaotic, sleepwalker's logic outside human ken.

As compared to Buffon's, Péret's *Natural History* is an anti-natural history drawn from observing environments much too complex and too alien to fit into storylines produced by a civilization anxious to keep *homo sapiens* at the apex of the evolutionary pyramid. In this age when computerized models used for mapping (and later, patenting, before finally invading) genomic patterns claim the ability to unlock the secrets of life itself, Péret's tales of mystery, imagination, and anarchy remind us all how one cannot control what is wild. Some environmentalists seek a world where nature engages with human nature in a dance of complementary unity rather than be locked in a death match for superiority as rivals, but surrealists are species traitors who continue to fight for and dream of a violent demolition of a universe where human civilization remains a value and a purpose.

An important first step in this direction is poetry that welds together the wilderness of the unconscious with the wildness of nature. The great surrealist poet Aimé Césaire asserted this very position from his tropical home in Martinique while the abominations of World War II befouled Europe, Africa, and Asia. "The unconscious that all true poetry calls upon is the receptacle of original relationships that bind us to nature," he wrote. "Within us, all the ages of humankind. Within us, animal, vegetable, mineral." The autocratic rationalism and scientific snobbery of Enlightenment celebrities like Buffon found its oh-so-logical conclusion in the sophisticated railroad timetables that crisscrossed the forests of Eastern Europe to supply the factories of concentration camps and the genie of technological atrocity unbottled at the Trinity proving grounds in New Mexican desert. Although he does not mention these things, Césaire implies them and more when he demands that people come to grips with "the superiority of the tree over humankind, of the tree that says 'yes' over a humankind who says 'no.' The superiority of the tree that is consent over a humankind who is evasiveness; the superiority of the tree which is rootedness and deepening over a humankind who is agitation and malfeasance. And that is why humankind does not blossom at all."[4]

In the early 1990s, surrealist poet-painter Penelope Rosemont applied Césaire's philosophy in a short essay that scans the headlines of the day and finds the correspondences linking the Los Angeles uprising, the fight to defend women's reproductive freedom, and the attempts to protect the spotted owl from extinction. "The struggle for women's reproductive rights—for *women's freedom*—is also the struggle for sexual freedom for all; and for the end of war, white supremacy and all oppression; for the glorious diversity of wildlife on a living Earth. We shall win or be defeated together."[5] This is vision of revolutionary equality where there are no hierarchies of priority or superiority, but rather a mutual, organic alliance for existence.

Despite the savage escalation in surveillance, harassment, and oppression by federal, state, and local police forces since 11 September 2001, the eco-resistance boldly continues to strike back against suburban sprawl, deforestation, agribusiness tyranny, and genetically-engineered crops. "We need no more words on the matter," Edward Abbey famously wrote. "Sentiment without action is the ruin of the soul. One brave deed is worth a thousand books."[6] But direct action without ideas can ruin more than the soul; we should always be on the lookout for new sentiments all the time, and continue to circulate them among ourselves in order to keep up with shifting topographies of direct action and State repression. Péret's *Natural History* may not appear to be as immediately utilitarian as the ELF's *Setting Fires With Electric Timers* or that handy manual to biotech crop-pulling, *The Nighttime Gardener*, but all efforts should be made to find a poetry that conveys a vision of wilderness that recognizes the necessity of emancipation—both esoteric and exoteric—from imposed, artificial constraints. As Romanticist revolutionary William Blake wrote, "Nature is Imagination itself."[7]

Notes

1. Benjamin Péret, *Le Déshonneur des poètes* (Mexico City: Poésie et revolution, 1945), 2. The first English language translation was by Cheryl Seaman and appeared in *Radical America* 4:6 (August 1970), 15-20.

2. Benjamin Péret, *Histoire naturelle* (Ussel [Haute-Corrèze, France]: [Jehan Mayoux] 1958). The essays, translated by Antony Melville and Marie-Louise Chenapan, are reprinted in Péret, *Death to the Pigs, and Other Writings* (Lincoln: University of Nebraska Press, 1988), 133-56.

3. Two posthumous publications on council communism by Benjamin Péret and Grandizo Munis, *Pour un second manifeste communiste* (Paris: Terrain vague, 1965) and *Les Syndicats contre la révolution* (Paris: Terrain vague, 1968), were influential in the uprisings of spring 1968.

4. Aimé Césaire, "Poetry and Knowledge," trans. by M. Richardson and K. Fijakowski, reprinted in Michael Richardson, ed. *Refusal of the Shadow: Surrealism and the Caribbean* (London: Verso, 1996), 139.

5. Penelope Rosemont, "Is it a Woman or a Bird or a Fire? [1992-3]," in Surrealist Experiences: *1001 Dawns, 221 Midnights* (Chicago: Black Swan Press, 2000), 163-4.

6. Edward Abbey, *Beyond the Wall: Essays from the Outside* (New York: Holt, Rinehart and Winston, 1984).

7. William Blake, letter to the Reverend Dr. Trusler (23 August 1799), in Geoffrey Keynes, ed., *William Blake. Complete Writings* (London: Oxford University Press, 1925).

WHAT'S THE USE OF WALKING IF THERE'S A FREIGHT TRAIN GOING YOUR WAY?—Black Hoboes & their Songs by Paul Garon. "A masterpiece of cultural history...this remarkable book disrupts common notions of what we mean by 'freedom' when it comes to black folk...Garon demonstrates that men and women who took to the road and their bards have much to teach us about America's 'bottom rail.'" —**Robin D. G. Kelley.** 288 pages, 25-track CD. Paper $27

HISTORY AGAINST MISERY. By David Roediger. Football strikes, the IWW, surrealism, May Day, hiphop, talk-radio, and writers as varied as André Breton, C.L.R. James, and Sterling Brown, this book focuses on the oppressive ideologies known as "miserabilism." *"A surrealist roadmap to liberated futures .... A book we must keep close to us as we struggle to overthrow misery once and for all"* —**Robin D.G. Kelley.** 184 pages. Profusely illustrated. Paper $17

LUCY PARSONS: Freedom, Equality & Solidarity— Writings & Speeches, 1878-1937, edited & introduced by Gale Ahren. Afterword by Roxanne Dunbar-Ortiz. First-ever anthology of tracts & talks (on anarchism, women, race, class war, the injustice system) by Lucy Parsons! Correcting several errors made by earlier writers, it adds much to our knowledge of Lucy and her relevance for freedom struggles today. 191 pages. Illustrated. $17

An Open Entrance to the Shut Palace of WRONG NUMBERS. By Franklin Rosemont. Drawings by Cruzeiro Seixas. Exploring the continuities and discontinuities between sleeping and waking, dream and reality, desire and necessity as manifested in misdialed telephone calls, Rosemont finds the Wrong Number not only a symptom of alienation but a symbol of the quest for true community, and also a disrupter of reified routine and thus a *lever* of change. *"About the cracking open of a* front in the revolution of everyday life. *Strangely endearing and exciting!"* —**Oliver Katz**. *"Opens a trail of investigation in the question of objective chance."* — **Guy Girard.** *"A reminder that surrealism is a force that remains afoot in the universe."* —**Laura Winton.** 187 pages. Paper $14

JOE HILL: The IWW & the Making of a Revolutionary Workingclass Counterculture, by Franklin Rosemont. A new in-depth study of the famous Wobbly bard, and of the IWW counterculture he came to personify. Details Hill's views on capitalism, race/gender issues, religion, and wilderness, as well as songwriting and his little-known work as cartoonist. *"Joe Hill has finally found a chronicler worthy of his revolutionary spirit, sense of humor, and poetic imagination"* —**Robin D. G. Kelley**. *"The best book ever on Joe Hill"* —**Utah Phillips**. *"Magnificent, practical, irreverent, magisterial: direct, passionate, sometimes funny, deeply searching"*— **Peter Linebaugh.** *"Rosemont seems to have hunted down every available detail of Hill's life and legend; he has spent decades accumulating IWW lore"*—**Michael Kazin, L. A. Times Book Review**. 656 pages. Illustrated. Cloth $35   Paper $22

DANCIN' IN THE STREETS! Anarchists, IWWs, Surrealists, Situationists & Provos in the 1960s. By Franklin Rosemont & Charles Radcliffe. This book is devoted to the far left of the far left. *The Rebel Worker,* a mimeo'd magazine started by young IWWs in 1964, multiracial and workingclass, inspired by IWW hobo wisdom, and also by surrealism. Critics derided them as "the left wing of the Beat Generation," but they were noted for their originality and uninhibited class-war humor and cartoons. *"Thanks for* Dancin'! *We surely need it!"* —**Diane di Prima**.*"Well worth reading"* — *Maximumrocknroll.* 450 pages. Paper $22   Cloth $25